MARGARET

Also by Kenneth Lonergan

Plays

This Is Our Youth
The Waverly Gallery
Lobby Hero

Screenplays

You Can Count on Me

Kenneth Lonergan

MARGARET

A Screenplay

Grove Press
New York

Printed in the United States of America
Published simultaneously in Canada

ISBN: 978-0-8021-2193-6
eBook ISBN: 978-0-8021-9298-1

Grove Press
an imprint of Grove/Atlantic, Inc.
154 West 14th Street
New York, NY 10011

Distributed by Publishers Group West

www.groveatlantic.com

13 14 15 16   10 9 8 7 6 5 4 3 2 1

For J.

Margaret: An Introduction
by Tony Kushner

Kenny Lonergan's *Margaret*, in its two film versions and now this screenplay, is enormously engaging and hugely entertaining. Its story unfolds on the printed page through dialogue that must occasion admiration, envy, and despair in every writer (or in me, at any rate) who tries to enlist the sounds and shapes of spontaneous utterance in creating music and meaning. On screen, Lonergan's magnificent script is married to achingly beautiful cinematography and that rare thing, an ensemble that is flawlessly, communally attuned to the film's subtle, ambivalent, complex, often-self-contradictory characters and the brilliantly observed world they inhabit. *Margaret* needs nothing more to recommend it as a great film than the way it so splendidly traces the difficult progress from adolescence towards adulthood, from heedless self-regard towards responsibility and connectedness.

So why introduce it? I was asked to do it by its writer and director, both of whom I greatly admire. How could I refuse? If an introduction is meant to encourage a potential reader, I hope I've done enough of that in the preceding paragraph, and perhaps I should stop here. But it seems to me that *Margaret* is one of those works of art possessed of a force that can't be accounted for by inventorying its many virtues, a force the unruly energy of which threatens the work's perfection. So I've taken this introduction as an opportunity to consider what makes *Margaret* so singular and unforgettable. *Margaret* isn't a perfect film; it's much better than that. *Margaret* is perfectly disturbing.

After a brief sampling of scenes from its teenage protagonist Lisa Cohen's everyday and rather ordinary life, a shocking event occurs in which Lisa is involved. It's violent and bloody, and it results in a woman dying. It's a little startling how immediately and abruptly Lisa and her family step back into everyday routine following the traumatic incident. We wait for the trauma to return, as we know it must.

But *Margaret*, relishing rather than editing out the messiness of life, doesn't schematize the journey from repression and denial towards awareness for the sake of constructing an easily traceable dramatic arc. The progress we hope Lisa is making towards assimilation, or some kind of negotiated peace, is cloudy, dodgy, nuanced, and not in any sense assured or certain. For one thing, the return of the repressed has to wage an ongoing fight with the everyday for time and space, a battle that lasts till the end of the story. Lisa has experienced something horrendous, but other stuff is happening and continues to happen: Her divorced mother has a big success as an actress and starts dating someone seriously; Lisa attends classes and parties, gets asked out on a date, speaks to her father on the phone as she prepares to go on a vacation with him.

The world, and the film's narrative structure, refuse to stop distracting us from Lisa's psychic journey, but external intrusions aren't the main source of our difficulty. The longer we watch Lisa struggle to find a way through the moment of horror she's stumbled into, the less confident we become about what sort of struggle we're watching. Is Lisa struggling to process the trauma, or is she struggling to experience it? Monica, the woman who dies in Lisa's arms, is a stranger; then again, I know of few scenes in film or onstage more intense than the two minutes or so Lisa spends with Monica before she dies. The nature of Lisa's connection to the dead stranger is something we, and Lisa herself, are left to guess at. We parse her subsequent behavior for clues, but we've spent only a little more time with Lisa than Lisa spends with Monica before Lisa is covered with Monica's blood, the blood of a woman for whose hideous demise she bears some responsibility. For the rest of the film, we feel that much of Lisa's misbehavior, miscalculations, manipulations, and mercurial emotionality is attributable to the guilt and grief that are fighting their way past her denials and into her consciousness and conscience, but to what extent? None of the people who theoretically know her well ascribe the often rude, hurtful, selfish things she does to the accident's aftermath. If her family, friends, or teachers feel she's behaving any worse than usual, they don't say it. Is she acting out because she's in mourning? Or is she using the mourning she should be feeling opportunistically? Is she mourning, or play-acting?

Lisa's an adolescent, and anyone who's spent time with one or remembers being one knows that there's no time of life more impossible than adolescence to distinguish with certainty what's real and what's performance. Alternating between vulnerability, naivety, dependency, transparency, legibility, honesty, and the unpleasant opposites of all those things, adolescents torment themselves and those in proximity to them, generating mutual irritation, if not to say raw antagonism. More than merely provoking us, adolescents pose a threat to our own sense of authenticity. Their unceasing, baffling fluctuations, from innocent ingenuousness to posturing and back again, infect us with doubt. We start to question what's real and what's performed in ourselves.

Since adolescence is a crucible we've all passed through, we know it ends; films about teenagers reassure of this fact, affording us relief tinged with a pleasant, nostalgic sadness for lost passion, pain, and incredible skin tone. But Lonergan's Lisa is not just any teenager. She's a traumatized, grieving, extremely bright, beautiful teenage daughter of an actress. Lisa is a handful, simultaneously recognizable and unknowable, familiar and strange, and *Margaret* an uncanny film.

That's another strange thing about *Margaret*: It's about a girl named Lisa. Lisa gets to star in her own movie, but not eponymously. That honor has been stolen from her by a much younger girl, whose tears for an autumn leaf-fall more than a hundred and fifty years ago inspired a remarkable and peculiar poem from Gerard Manley Hopkins, convert to Catholicism and a Jesuit (there's a theological discussion to be had about *Margaret*, but to wander into it would be to overstay my welcome).

In the film we hear and get to watch Lisa listen to the poem—the full text of which is in this version of the screenplay on page 152. The poet begins by asking the young girl, Margaret, who it is she's mourning for; he concludes by answering his question, and his answer is "Margaret." When John, Lisa's teacher, finishes reading the poem, he provides another example of the prodigiously improbable task of teaching anything, or of knowing what you're teaching, that accumulate throughout the film. After the arhythmic, alliterative, tongue-tying pell-mell of Hopkins's odd, often telegraphic lines ("What heart heard of, ghost guessed"), formidable enough for a reader and nearly incomprehensible to a listener, have flown at, around, and past Lisa, her classmates, and us, John asks, "Any thoughts?"

I have a few thoughts, John. Maybe the poem's about Margaret grieving at the apprehension of her own mortality, and, along the way, she's grieving for the imminent death-by-coarsening of the tenderhearted child she presently is, someone who can cry when leaves die in autumn. Although the poem opens with a question and ends with an answer, the last couplet seems at odds with itself: Is Margaret mourning for a shared human condition, "the blight that man was born for," or for herself, specific and alone, as the final line rather abruptly states? When he declares that "it is Margaret you mourn for," is Hopkins accusing this young child of solipsism? The same sort of solipsism Lisa is accused of by Emily, her middle-aged partner in pursuing justice for Monica and resolution for herself? Are Margaret and Lisa exploiting something grand and sad but unrelated to them, for the purpose of borrowing significance to help them experience sorrow, or to help advertise the importance of their own unhappiness?

Hopkins's final line, in the film's context, raises for Lisa and for us at least the specter of self-aggrandizing fakery. She isn't mourning for Monica's death; she's using it to mourn her own, relatively minor sorrows.

Emily's splendid anti-fakery splenetic, when it finally explodes in Lisa's surprised face, is so gratifying! The perpetually astonishing Emily—a wholly original, unexpected, essential creation—provides those of us who've been watching *Margaret* with a much needed release for our vexation, satisfying our need to halt Lisa's variability and flatten her complexity. Emily answers one of the film's main questions as strongly—one mustn't say *stridently*!—as Hopkins answers his poem's.

But the film won't provide us with easy satisfactions, because life never does. Our relief at Emily's repudiation of Lisa is haunted by a sense of unfairness, and even disappointment. No character other than Emily has shown him- or herself competent at assuming adult authority; she instantly occupies the moral center of *Margaret* and holds her place there, for a time, until her thunderbolt outburst at Lisa. However understandable, however satisfying, Emily's rough handling and forcible eviction of Lisa is inappropriate, out of control. Lisa's a pain in the ass, but she's a teenager. And isn't Emily in fact a little strident? Or even if she isn't, so what, what's the big deal? Lisa is a teenager, and this reaction, it's too much.

Thus Emily stands down from the film's moral center, leaving it the void, or rather the busy unmonitored intersection it was before she arrived. *Margaret* is noticeably lacking in reliably grown-up grownups. John, the English teacher, is overmastered in his own classroom by an iconoclast student who's either an airhead or hostile, and when he attempts to lay down the law after he stumbles across Lisa and another student brazenly smoking pot, he's defeated by his inability to reconcile being the girls' teacher and wanting to be their peer, retreating, mortified by their giggling. Lisa's favorite teacher, the boyish Mr. Aaron, permits cheating, seems even more boyish riding his bike, lives in a sublet that looks like a dorm room, and . . . well, it gets worse; read the script.

The failings of Lisa's teachers and parent-surrogates to adhere to adulthood are all the more lamentable because her parents, if anything, fail even more resoundingly. Early in the film, Lisa's mother, Joan, actually regresses, upon request, from an adult to a child (Shirley Temple) to a gurgling infant. She snaps out of it, but she never goes the distance to an acceptable parental stability. A professional actress with an appetite for histrionics, she calls her daughter a "little cunt" when provoked, and, when driven to exasperation, throws not only a fit but food and flatware. She isn't a grotesque; Lonergan's gifts for intimacy and empathy are too prodigious to make caricatures instead of characters. Joan is distressing because she's so easy to identify with. She's a thoroughly decent, likable woman, just more thin-skinned and insecure, more self-pitying and less resilient, than is ideal in a divorced single working mother of two teenagers.

When Lisa gets pregnant, she immediately tells her mother. This scene, omitted from the theatrical version of the film, but included in the extended cut available on DVD, is perhaps my favorite. I think it contains much of *Margaret* in magically economical miniature.

JOAN

OK. What do you want to do?

LISA

What do you mean? Aren't you going to *tell* me what to do? (*Half-laughing*) Baby . . .?

JOAN

It's your body. It's your baby. What do you want to do?

JOAN

Yes! Now who is the father?

LISA

It could be a lot of people.

Lisa's in trouble, and she turns to her mother for help. Joan, of course, immediately tosses responsibility back at her daughter. Lisa responds by making her plea for help more explicit, and, I think for the first time in the film, protests the failure of the adults around her to take care of her. Joan comes back with bromides, entrenching herself in an abrogation of parental duty.

Lisa's follow-up, "*Baby* . . . ?" is prefaced, onscreen and in the screenplay, by a half-laugh. She's indignantly upbraiding Joan for using "baby" to refer to a first-trimester fetus, reflexively and probably protectively invoking pro-choice politics and vigilantly monitored political correctness. She's also protecting herself from the incomprehensible news Joan's just delivered: There's an actual *baby* on the way. At no point in the film is Lisa more poignantly helpless, more infuriatingly, shockingly clueless—in other words, more age-appropriate. Lisa is a child, a pregnant child, in serious need of mothering.

She's in need of fathering, too, as Joan's next line serves to remind us. After impatiently affirming/insisting on the possibility of a real infant making its improbable way into this world of semi-infantilized adults, Joan continues to dodge Lisa's plea for maternal control by trying to change the subject to the absent father. Lisa's non-answer, suggesting sexual profligacy, repays Joan's maternal dereliction beautifully. But "It could be a lot of people" is equally a beautifully vague description of Lisa's own faraway father, Karl Cohen, decamped to the opposite coast.

Karl is in intermittent telephone contact with his daughter. Their conversation is excruciatingly out of kilter. Lisa tries harder to connect with her father than with almost anyone else; Karl responds with half-hearted bonhomie, feeble, flickering consternation and an inappropriate overinvestment in his daughter's sex life, with creepily terrible advice thrown in regarding her dating technique—advice compounded of his anger at the women who got away and the high school dateless dweeb he was and has never outgrown being.

Nearly everyone we meet in *Margaret* has a claim on our sympathies. Joan's deficiencies haven't diminished her immense, apparently indestructible love for her children, and her refusal to surrender their relationship to her punishingly rejecting daughter becomes, finally, heroic. Even the crass, greedy Berwitzes have a history of combat over finances with their dead relative, who, from her best friend's description, sounds like a formidable foe, and probably Rob and Abigail have their own version of the fight with Monica over their children's trust fund. Karl is one of only two characters whose conduct is inexcusable (which is not to say incomprehensible—again, in Lonergan's work, even inexcusable behavior is uncomfortably comprehensible).

If we look for the familial drama absorbed and metaphorized within Lisa's appropriation of Monica's tragedy—a reading endorsed by Emily and by Lisa herself, first in her dream and then as she begins to give way to heartbreak at the end of the film—Joan is Monica, the bloodied victim, while Karl is the bus driver, Maretti, the other inexcusable character, catastrophically irresponsible, who may escape justice.

What's inexcusable is in legal terms called a crime, and demands justice in the form of punishment. However discontinuous her search or overdetermined her motives, Lisa is searching for justice and tries to act as its agent. She shares in the guilt, so she's also searching for just punishment for herself. She's searching for responsibility.

In *Margaret*, progress in justice and ethics are inseparably intertwined with the corkscrew and retrograde processes of human development. Immaturity and irresponsibility are more than sociologically and psychologically analyzable in *Margaret*;

they're moral phenomena as well, and their prolongation results in injustice, with bloody consequences.

It isn't justice that ultimately arrives, but a shabby deal that satisfies no moral imperatives and no one other the MTA, the undeserving Berwitzes, and probably Maretti. Emily, with her prophylactically reduced adult expectations, will wince and go on. But for Lisa it's a shattering, cataclysmic failure, the revelation of a tragic flaw in the design of the universe. Heartbroken, she flees from it, from the death of the possibility of justice, of expiation, of clarity, of a reconciled and undivided world.

I've watched *Margaret* a number of times, but it wasn't till I read the screenplay that I noticed that Lisa is a student at Ralph Waldo Emerson High School, "one of the few remaining Manhattan '60s-inspired progressive schools." I'd never heard of this school, so I googled. It doesn't exist; Lonergan made it up. So why'd he name his made-up school in honor of Emerson?

Perhaps he was thinking about the famous passage in Emerson's essay, "Experience," written two years after the death of his five-year-old son. Arguably the bleakest words Emerson wrote, it's impossible to not hear the brokenhearted despair beneath the ashy surface.

> People grieve and bemoan themselves, but it is not half so bad with them as they say. There are moods in which we court suffering, in the hope that here, at least, we shall find reality, sharp peaks and edges of truth. But it turns out to be scene-painting and counterfeit. The only thing grief has taught me, is to know how shallow it is. That, like all the rest,

plays about the surface, and never introduces me into the reality, for contact with which, we would even pay the costly price of sons and lovers. Was it Boscovich who found out that bodies never come in contact? Well, souls never touch their objects. An innavigable sea washes with silent waves between us and the things we aim at and converse with. Grief too will make us idealists. In the death of my son, now more than two years ago, I seem to have lost a beautiful estate,—no more. I cannot get it nearer to me. If tomorrow I should be informed of the bankruptcy of my principal debtors, the loss of my property would be a great inconvenience to me, perhaps, for many years; but it would leave me as it found me,—neither better nor worse. So is it with this calamity: it does not touch me: some thing which I fancied was a part of me, which could not be torn away without tearing me, nor enlarged without enriching me, falls off from me, and leaves no scar. It was caducous. I grieve that grief can teach me nothing, nor carry me one step into real nature.

Caducous, to spare you a visit to the dictionary, is a botanical term meaning "liable to fall."

If *Margaret* is asking the dangerous question, "For whom do you mourn?" Emerson replies that it is impossible for anyone to mourn anyone else. Our own individual deaths, he concludes in the essay, are "the only realit[ies] that will not dodge us."

In the aggrieved tone of the passage from "Experience," in his distaste for and distrust of "scene-painting and counterfeit," Emerson's seems a kindred spirit of Emily's. But it must be said that Emily doesn't grasp the mysterious relationship between performance and the real. How could she? She says she almost never goes to the theater.

She'd find only further confirmation that Lisa's grief is mostly teenaged sound and fury if she'd been able to watch Lisa as she barely pauses to absorb the aborting of her baby, I mean her *baby* . . .?, before she turns it into a showy bit of stagecraft performed for an audience of Mr. Aaron and a female teacher. But Lisa's dramatizing, here as elsewhere, is fakery that's not *only* fake. The flailing artifice of Lisa's brief performance metes out a small measure of punitive justice to Mr. Aaron, and serves as a confession, the humiliation of which is expiation for what may be a crime, or even a sin (Gerard Manley Hopkins would call it that) —unquestionably for something with bloody consequences. Drama, as Shakespeare, Brecht, and many others have pointed out, is where the familiar and the strange cohabitate with and transform one another, with consequences not genuinely bloody, and not exactly palpable, but nonetheless real.

And the theater is where *Margaret* leads us, and leaves us. Courtesy of a dead man Joan is grieving for and also trying to grieve for, mother and daughter go to the Met. They attend a performance of *Tales of Hoffmann,* an opera the history of which is almost as difficult, almost as full of suffering and torture and near-brushes with oblivion as the travails that made *Margaret*'s postproduction life the stuff of legend. Offenbach's opera exists today among several surviving iterations, like *Margaret* does, like many great works of art do when, wedding the everyday to the unknown, the familiar to the strange, they attain a posterity as perpetually unsettled as unsettling.

Lonergan couldn't have known how rough the road would be between his last day of shooting and the film's first public screening six years later, so their similarly tempestuous careers can't explain why he chose *Tales of Hoffmann* for *Margaret*'s last scene. The hero of the opera is E.T.A. Hoffmann, the writer from whose peculiar writings Freud derived his theory of the uncanny; Hoffmann reveals the *unheimlich*, the strange, lurking in the darker corners of the *heimlich*, the home-like, the familiar, and it gives us a shivery access to a lost morbidity casting shadows in our infancy. Whether Hoffmann and Freud informed Lonergan's choice is something only he knows. Maybe he chose the opera because he loved the fourth-act opener, "The Barcarolle." Who doesn't?

Joan and Lisa certainly learn to. Onstage, two singing actresses serenade one another, one of the actresses playing a woman (and author's muse) who's playing a man. It's as artificial as anything can be, and it draws forth tears from Lisa, and then from Joan, as we watch them watching Nicklausse and Giulietta sing about love and loss.

And as we watch, scene-painting and counterfeit work their magic. There's a reconciliation between Lisa and her mother. And here the screenplay parts company with the two versions of the film.

Lonergan ends his screenplay with Lisa and Joan making a tentative connection, taking a first step. Lisa cries, then Joan cries; then they hold and squeeze each other's hands.

In the film versions, Joan and Lisa fall into a full embrace, holding each other, sobbing. It's a decidedly strange moment. The embrace is startling, a little too much for members of an audience, a Met audience anyway. And though we see that some manner of transformation is occurring, some progress is being made for Lisa and Joan, it also seems a little . . . theatrical?

Can they really be so oblivious to those around them? Is this extravagant public gesture the cause or the effect of what they're feeling? If the feelings breaking through are powerful enough to pull them out of the Met and into a private place, what are those feelings? Regret, relief, love? All or none of the above? Loss?

The screenplay helps us guess at what Joan is feeling without telling us too much. In words that invoke fairy tales and witches, that could have come from E.T.A. Hoffmann, she's "grateful finally that the spell has been broken."

And what is Lisa feeling? The last words of the script—*The duet ends. CUT TO BLACK.*—leave us in the dark, wondering as ever why she's crying. What are her tears for? For which of many occasions? For remorse, for which loss? We only know that she cries, generating questions, holding her mother, or only her mother's hand. Are their souls touching? Or are they supporting one another in her separate grief?

Who are they mourning for?

Author's Note

This is the shooting script of my movie, *Margaret*—more or less. It includes a number of scenes that I deleted from the picture, and retains the original versions of several scenes that were shortened. There are also a few sections in the two incarnations of the finished film where the scene ordering was changed. But in most of those sections, I stuck with what's in the movie, and adjusted the screenplay instead. However, there are one or two re-ordered sequences where I honestly couldn't say which works better. Since the movie is there to be watched, in those instances where both versions seemed equally interesting, I retained the scene order from the original screenplay here.

You can rewrite or adjust a play for as long as you're alive and able to write, if you want to. But a movie is locked and frozen and will never be adjusted again, in most cases. Which is probably for the best. But while there's not much material here that I would be likely to reinstate in the body of the movie even if I could, I still like a lot of the deleted scenes just as scenes. It's also perfectly possible I cut out some pieces of the story I should have left in—even if it doesn't seem that way to me at the moment. In any case, I am happy for the chance to include most of them in this edition, since they were there at the beginning and are unlikely to appear anywhere else.

Kenneth Lonergan
New York City, 2013

Cast List

Lisa Cohen	Anna Paquin
Joan	J. Smith-Cameron
Emily	Jeannie Berlin
Ramon	Jean Reno
Mr. Aaron	Matt Damon
Maretti	Mark Ruffalo
John	Matthew Broderick
Monica Patterson	Allison Janney
Paul	Kieran Culkin
Abigail	Betsy Aidem
Darren	John Gallagher Jr.
Becky	Sarah Steele
Angie	Hina Abdullah
Curtis	Cyrus Hernstadt
Detective Mitchell	Stephen Adly Guirgis

Deutsch	Jonathan Hadary
Dave the Lawyer	Michael Ealy
Mrs. Maretti	Rosemarie DeWitt
Gary	T. Scott Cunningham
2nd AIS Detective	Kevin Geer
1st Man at Accident	Glenn Fleshler
2nd Man at Accident	Stephen Conrad Moore
Kid at Accident	Gio Perez
1st Neighborhood Lady	Anna Berger
2nd Neighborhood Lady	Rose Arrick
Bonnie	Enid Graham
Mr. Klein	Jerry Matz
Mr. Lewis	Kevin Carroll
Karl	Kenneth Lonergan
Annette	Kelly Wolf
Victor	Josh Hamilton
David	Jake O'Connor
Lionel	David Mazzucchi
Kirsten	Jessica Dunphy
Leslie	Brittany Underwood
Matthew	Nick Grodin
Monica	Olivia Thirlby
Anthony	Adam Rose
Kurt	Matt Bush
Rob	Adam LeFevre

Rodrigo	Carlo Alban
Neighbor in Elevator	Johann Carlo
Opera Fan	Pippin Parker
Woman Mourner	Stephanie Cannon
Nurse	Liza Colón-Zayas
Salesgirl	Krysten Ritter
Young Cop (not photographed)	Jason Pendergraft
"Hoffman" Conductor	Yves Abel
Actress in John's Play	Breanna Pine
Giuletta (Soprano) in *Hoffman*	Renée Fleming
Nicklausse (Mezzo Soprano) in *Hoffman*	Susan Graham
Norma (Soprano) in *Norma*	Christine Goerke

EXT. NEW YORK CITY—MIDTOWN. AUTUMN, 2002. DAY.

A crowded corner full of New Yorkers step off the curb and into the crosswalk—Before the first foot lands on the street we go to SUPER SLOW MOTION as the midday work crowd crosses the street.

EXT. NEW YORK CITY STREETS. DAY.

MONTAGE—Slow motion shots of New Yorkers, midday, all kinds, going all different ways, all over the city.

CREDITS END.

EXT. CENTRAL PARK WEST. DAY.

WIDE ON: The Central Park Reservoir and the great buildings of the Upper West Side beyond, as seen through the old chain-link fence on the opposite side of the Park.

INT. HIGH SCHOOL CLASSROOM. DAY.

An 11th-grade math class at the Ralph Waldo Emerson School, one of the few remaining Manhattan '60s-inspired progressive schools. About twenty kids, mostly white secular Jewish. A sprinkling of black and Hispanic kids. The teacher, MR. AARON, late 20s, and very handsome, is returning test papers.

                    MR. AARON
          Abrams . . . Allende . . .

One after the other the students get up to collect their tests, glance at the results, and drag themselves back to their chairs.

ON LISA COHEN, just 17. Not the best-looking girl in her class but definitely in the top five. She listens listlessly, somewhat bad-temperedly.

MR. AARON

Bernstein . . . Cohen . . .

At "Cohen" LISA gets up and heads for the desk.

LISA'S POV, closing in slowly on Mr. Aaron. He glances up as she approaches. Their eyes meet. He has a no-nonsense expression on his face. As she reaches out for her test:

LISA

Thank you, Mr. Aaron.

She walks back. On her test he's written: **B– "SEE ME!"**

INT. HIGH SCHOOL CLASSROOM. DAY. LATER.

AFTER CLASS—The last students go out as Mr. Aaron gestures for Lisa to take a seat.

MR. AARON

Take a seat, Lisa. I just wanna talk about your
test for a minute.

LISA
(*Sitting*)

Sure.

MR. AARON

Now . . . I know you had a little help . . .

LISA

Well—I mean—I didn't *cheat*, if that's what you mean.

MR. AARON

I'm just saying I know you had a little help.

LISA

A lot of people did.

MR. AARON

Be that as it may—

LISA

I mean, I'll take it over again if you want, but like, what would be the point? It's not like I'm ever gonna actually need to *know* this stuff in my daily *life*...

MR. AARON

Well, Lisa, that's just not necessarily true. Haven't you ever developed an interest in something you didn't initially think you were going to develop an interest in?

LISA

Um, no, not really.

Mr. Aaron looks down for a moment to hide his amusement. Lisa looks at him with secret adoration. He looks up.

LISA

Anyway, it *was* open *book.* So what's the big difference between using a *book* and like, I don't
know, using somebody else's *mind* who's like,
really good at *math?* It's not like this person
did the whole test for me.

MR. AARON

Oh no?

LISA

No. I did some of it.

She smiles at him. He is no longer smiling back.

MR. AARON

Well, next time I'd appreciate it if you did all
of it. OK?

LISA

You are so fair.

INT. SCHOOL HALLWAY. DAY.

*TRACKING LISA from behind as she walks through the halls past
her fellow students. She walks through a door—*

EXT. ALLEY. DAY—CONTINUOUS.

*—where kids are smoking. Lots of butts on the ground. The walls
covered with graffiti. Lisa goes to her friend BECKY and takes out her
cigarettes. A kid named KURT smokes nearby.*

> BECKY

What did he say to you?

> LISA

Nothing . . . Mr. Aaron and I have an understanding about my math problem.

Becky laughs. Lisa laughs.

> LISA

He is *so* appealing.

*A long-haired kid comes out, followed by a somewhat preppier girl,
KIRSTEN, and her look-alike friend LESLIE.*

> KIRSTEN

OK, Mr. Ferrar is such an asshole.

> KURT

What'd he do, call on you?

> KIRSTEN

Fuck *you,* Kurt.

> LESLIE

Kirsten is really upset.

> KURT

I'm sorry.

> KIRSTEN
> *(To Leslie)*

Let me have one of those, will you?

Leslie gives Kirsten a cigarette and lights it for her.

BECKY

Kirsten, I didn't know you smoked.

KIRSTEN

I don't. I'm just really angry. (*To Leslie*) Check
out what he said to me last *week.*

*She drops her voice. They whisper and then both laugh. Lisa watches
them.*

LESLIE

Are you serious?

Lisa overhears MONICA, *a pretty, elegant 11th-grader, talking to some
other girls seated on the steps.*

MONICA

. . . I just don't think you can really know a guy
until you've slept with him.

Lisa, listening, is not so sure, but wouldn't know.

INT. AMERICAN HISTORY CLASS. DAY.

The class is taught by two teachers; MR. KLEIN, *50s, and* MR. LEWIS,
*30s. On the blackboard are scrawled the words "STRIKERS,"
"PINKERTONS," and "PREZ. McKINLEY."*

KLEIN

. . . So the President of the United States, Wil-
liam B. McKinley, authorized the use of private
detectives to break the strike, and they went out

there and shot them down! Just like they did
in Virginia, just like they did in Pennsylvania.
Because they did not care! They did not care!

LEWIS
(*Low, rumbling*)

And that's basically it . . . That's basically all
there is to say.

KLEIN

All right? Go ahead, uhhhhh: Becky!

BECKY

Well, Mr. Klein . . . I mean, was there ever a
good President of the United States?

There is some laughter from the students.

KLEIN

I don't know, Becky. I think that's a good question. What do you think? You. Lionel. What do
you think? Did we ever have a good President?

LIONEL

Um . . . I don't know. I guess most of them have
just been totally corrupt.

LEWIS

Lisa?

LISA

Can I just say, I'm not necessarily like a big
fan of all the Presidents of the United States,

especially the current one, but I still don't
think it's necessarily all that useful to categorize
every President as universally corrupt, because
that just seems very general to me. Especially
if you're going to judge them by the standard
of—whatever they're supposed to traditionally
be *like* in some mythical version of America that
probably never existed to begin with.

ANTHONY, an intellectual smart-ass, leans back in his chair.

ANTHONY

Lisa has raised a salient point.

There are some laughs from the class.

EXT. SCHOOL. DAY.

*School is letting out. Lisa walks away from the building. A short
energetic kid named DARREN falls in step with her.*

DARREN

Hey, how'd you do?

LISA

Oh hey, Darren. It was fine. Thank you *so much*.

DARREN

So he didn't give you a hard time or anything?

LISA

Well, he knows I'm not planning to like, go
into *mathematics* or anything . . . He was totally
cool about it. He's *so* cool.

DARREN

Oh yeah, everybody loves Mr. *Aaron.*

LISA

What's that supposed to mean?

DARREN

Nothing. The man is very lovable.

They stop at the corner.

DARREN

What are you doing now?

LISA

I was gonna go look for a cowboy hat.

DARREN

Why would you want to buy a *cowboy* hat?

LISA

Because my dad is supposed to take me and
my brother to this ranch in New Mexico to go
horseback riding, and I don't think it would be
right to appear on horseback in New Mexico
without the appropriate equestrian parapher-
nalia, Darren. You wouldn't understand these
things.

DARREN

That is a definite possibility.

LISA

Anyway . . . Thanks again . . .

DARREN

Before you venture forth on your bizarre quest
for a cowboy hat . . . ?

LISA

Yes, Darren?

DARREN

. . . what are you up to later? Like tonight.

LISA

I don't know.

DARREN

You wanna go to a movie?

LISA

What do you mean, like on a date?

DARREN

No, not on a date, just go to a movie.
I don't know if it's a fucking date!

LISA

All right. Calm down. What do you wanna see?

DARREN

I don't know, I don't even know what's playing!
I don't know if it's a date! Let's just forget it!

I hate the fuckin' movies anyway. They're just
bullshit. They're all bullshit.

LISA

OK, take it easy, I was just asking! I'm sorry!

DARREN

What if it was a date, anyway? Would that be
so horrendous?

LISA

Oh my God. Are you like—are you asking me
out? (*Pause*) Are you? (*Pause*) Hello . . . ? Earth
to Darren.

DARREN

I don't know. Yeah. I mean . . . I feel like we're
already really close . . .

LISA

Oh my God . . .

DARREN

. . . and I think we'd be a really good
match—What?

LISA

Nothing. This is—Nothing.

DARREN

So—Yeah. I would. I mean, yes. I am. Yes I am.

LISA

Wow. I mean—I am *really* flattered. But I would definitely not want to do anything to mess up our friendship.

DARREN

I view this as a way of *strengthening* our friendship.

LISA

It would definitely *change* it . . .

DARREN

I know: It's a fairly dangerous move.

LISA

Well . . . I would definitely have to think about this . . .

DARREN

Absolutely. Give it some thought.

LISA

OK, I will.

Pause. He is looking at her like he wants something.

LISA

Why do you look like that?

DARREN

Like what?

LISA

What do you want from me?

DARREN

Not a thing!

LISA

All right. I'll see you later.

DARREN

All right.

She turns and walks away, pleased by the conversation.

EXT. LISA'S STREET—WEST '80S. DAY.

Lisa walks down her street and lets herself into the prewar apartment building.

INT. COHEN APARTMENT. DAY.

She lets herself into the narrow apartment. A long hall covered with framed pictures, photographs, and play posters opens onto a cramped living room crammed with books, plays, and magazines. A stereo, TV, and computer are stuck in the corners. Beyond this is the kitchen and another hallway leading to the bathrooms and bedrooms.

LISA

Hello . . . !

INT. KITCHEN. CONTINUOUS.

Lisa comes in, drops her bag, opens the refrigerator. She gets out some cold pizza and sits down with it. Her brother CURTIS, 11, comes in.

> CURTIS
>
> Hi.

> LISA
>
> Is Mom home?

> CURTIS
>
> She went to the store.

INT. LIVING ROOM. DAY.

Curtis is practicing the piano.

INT. LISA'S MOTHER'S BEDROOM.

Lisa, on her cell phone, rummages in her mother's bureau. During the following she finds a small supply of cash and steals forty dollars.

> LISA
> (*On the phone*)
>
> What are you up to tonight? . . . Nothing: Darren wants me to go to the movies with him. You want to come? . . . I guess around eight?

EXT. BROADWAY. DAY.

POV LISA: slowly passing by Broadway clothing store windows. No cowboy hats. She walks down Broadway window-shopping, enjoying herself.

EXT. ANTIQUE CLOTHING STORE. DAY.

Through the window, we see Lisa talk to the pretty, mid-20s SALESGIRL *with an embroidered cowboy hat.*

EXT. BROADWAY. DAY.

Lisa slowly passes by and looks in various store windows. She stops and looks at some shoes.

REFLECTED IN THE WINDOW, behind her, a city BUS pulls up to a bus stop and wheezes as the doors open.

EXT./INT. STREET/BUS. SIMULTANEOUS.

The BUS DRIVER is wearing a cowboy hat. He is in his 30s and very good-looking. Past the disembarking passengers we see Lisa's back as she scans the shoe store.

ON LISA—She turns around and sees the Bus Driver. She sees his cowboy hat and just as the doors shut—

> LISA
> *(To Driver)*

Hey!

The bus lurches away. Lisa takes off after it.

IN THE BUS—CLOSE on the Bus Driver, oblivious to Lisa, who we can see out the door and window, falling behind.

ON THE STREET—The bus falls behind a slow-moving car, and Lisa catches up.

IN THE BUS—Lisa appears at the bus doors, waving and calling out. The Bus Driver sees her, smiles, and waves back.

ON THE STREET—Lisa is running alongside the bus.

LISA

Hey! Where'd you get your cowboy hat?

IN THE BUS—The Bus Driver can't hear her, but smiles at her with good-natured flirtatiousness.

ON THE STREET—The LIGHT at the curb turns YELLOW.

THE SLOW-MOVING CAR in front of the bus floors it to make the light.

The Bus Driver sees his way is clear and steps on the gas. He turns and waves goodbye to Lisa. She points at her head and then at him. He smiles, not quite getting it.

The LIGHT turns RED.

Still looking at Lisa, the Bus Driver lifts the hat off his head in a farewell salute as—

Lisa sees the bus pass under the RED LIGHT—

An Upper West Side woman, early 50s (later identified as MONICA PATTERSON), holding some grocery bags, steps off the curb between two cars to cross Broadway.

VERY FAST:

The Bus Driver turns his head to look straight forward.

POV BUS DRIVER—Monica is directly in front of him.

POV MONICA—The bus roars up at her.

The Bus Driver slams on the BRAKES.

POV LISA—Monica is clipped by the huge bus and pulled, tumbling underneath.

Lisa SCREAMS. Pedestrians all over turn around.

Monica is pulled and crunched in a horrible twisting tumble.

Everything stops.

TRACKING LISA fast as she runs across the street toward the accident. As she gets closer she sees Monica's leg sticking out from under the bus.

Then with some confusion, she realizes that Monica herself is right in front of her, and that her blood is spreading everywhere. Monica is reaching out vaguely, unable to speak. She is making choking sounds.

Lisa stands over her for a second, frozen. She crouches down and tries to do something but doesn't know what to do, where to put her hands. Other people start converging.

IN THE BUS—The Bus Driver puts the bus in Park, opens the door, and rushes out.

WE TRACK him as he comes around to where a crowd has already formed. He hangs back on the outside, but we break through till we find Lisa kneeling next to the disoriented Monica, holding her hand. They are both covered in blood. Several other people are shouting and talking all at once.

1ST MAN

Somebody call an ambulance! Call an ambulance! Everyone calm down!

KID

I'm calling one right now . . . !

The Kid is already dialing his cell phone. Other people are doing the same.

2ND MAN

Get an ambulance!

1ST MAN

Someone's calling one!

LISA

Ma'am, can you hear me? Can you hear me?

MONICA

I don't know. Where am I? What is going on?

LISA	1ST MAN
You're on Broadway and 75th Street in New York— New York—You were in a bad accident—	Don't try to talk! You don't have to talk—

MONICA	2ND MAN
Who are you?	Never mind, let her talk—

LISA

My name is Lisa.

MONICA

What do you mean? Am I dead?

LISA

No, you're not dead. You were in a traffic accident, but you're gonna be OK—

MONICA

What do you mean? What happened?

LISA

You were run over by a bus.

MONICA

You've got to be kidding me. A bus?

LISA
(*Almost laughs*)

Yeah—!

1ST MAN

Is anyone a doctor? Could
we get a doctor?

MONICA

So where am I now? Who
are you?

2ND MAN

Is there a doctor anywhere?

LISA

We're on Broadway and 75th
Street. You don't know me—

*The onlookers are all talking at once, shouting for doctors, calling
911, etc.*

MONICA

I don't understand. Is it still happening?

LISA

No—I mean yes—The accident is over, but I
think you're a little confused—

MONICA

I'll say I'm confused—

1ST MAN

Here, lemme try to see if I can—

He tries to detach Lisa's hand from Monica's. Monica SCREAMS.

MONICA

NO! Don't let go of me!

LISA	2ND MAN
I'm not, I'm not gonna let go—	She needs a tourniquet or she's going to die.

MONICA	1ST MAN
Don't let go of me!	OK, let me just—

The 1st Man pulls back Monica's blood-soaked shirt—He is sprayed by a jet of blood from a severed artery. Everyone recoils and shouts.

1ST MAN	2ND MAN
Jesus Christ!	Oh my God . . . !

MONICA

Oh my God what's happening to me!

LISA

You're gonna be all right!
The ambulance is on its
way! Just hold on until they
get here!

MONICA

Thank you, honey. Just
don't let go of me.

LISA

I won't. I swear. They just
want to put a tourniquet on
you.

1ST MAN

I'm sorry! I'm just trying
to—we're trying to put a
tourniquet on you.

2ND MAN

We need to get a tourniquet
on you. (*To 1st Man*) Do
you have a belt? We can use
your belt.

1ST MAN

I can't even see where to—
(*Takes off his belt*)

MONICA

What do you mean? Are they doctors? Who
are they?

LISA

No—they're not doctors.
They were just passing by.

1ST MAN

I can't even see—

MONICA

Well, get 'em the fuck away from me!!!

1ST MAN

Ma'am, we're only trying to help you!

2ND MAN

Never mind that! Try it higher up. Try to put
it higher up!

1ST MAN

You wanna do it? You know what to do. Why
don't you do it?

LISA
(*To the 1st Man*)

Are you kidding me!?

MONICA

I can't see anything. Are my eyes open or
closed?

*This silences everyone. Lisa looks at the 1st Man. He shakes his head,
panicked; he doesn't know what to say.*

LISA
(*To Monica*)

They're open.

MONICA
(*Starts to cry*)

What do you mean?

LISA	2ND MAN
You were in a terrible accident! But you're going to be fine, so just hang on!	I'll try it. You want me to try it?

> 1ST MAN
>
> Hold on a second, I think I got it.

> 2ND MAN
>
> Just put it higher up! Just move it—

> KID
>
> Try putting it higher up!

> 1ST MAN
>
> There's nowhere to put it! I can't even—

Lisa looks at the incredible amount of blood still spreading everywhere, all over her, all over the street.

> LISA
>
> WILL SOMEBODY CALL THE FUCKING AMBULANCE!?!

> 1ST MAN
>
> Calm down! We already called them! So just calm down!

> 2ND MAN
>
> Take it easy!

> KID
>
> I called them two minutes ago, and somebody else probably called them too!

> LISA
>
> Well they're obviously not coming fast enough so maybe you should call them *again*! Why not call them *again*!?

> MONICA
>
> Could somebody call my daughter?

LISA

Sure—! We can call her. What's her name?

KID

You want my phone?

1ST MAN

OK, OK, hold on.

LISA

Tell me her name and give
me her—

2ND MAN

You got it. Just pull it
around. Here—

MONICA

It's Lisa.

1ST MAN

It's OK—

KID

I got a cell phone, you want me to call her?

LISA

It's—No—that's my name. Is that your daughter's name?

MONICA

What? What are you talking about?

LISA
(*On 2nd "what"*)

I'm s—I'm not trying to be confusing. My name
is Lisa: Is that your daughter's name?

MONICA

Jesus Christ, would you call her? Just *call* her!

LISA

I can't call her if you don't give me the
number—!

1ST MAN

I got it. I got it!

*He's managed to make a tourniquet with his belt around Monica's
upper thigh—out of frame.*

2ND MAN

Ma'am? You're gonna be OK.

KID

You're gonna be OK!

LISA

What's your daughter's number?

Monica starts breathing a horrible, rattling choking.

MONICA

Sweetie . . . I don't think I'm gonna make it.

LISA

Oh no, please hang on. The ambulance is
gonna be here any *minute!*

Monica dies.

LISA

Oh please hang on! Please hang on!

1ST MAN

OK. It's OK. She's gone.

The 1st Man tries to pull her away.

LISA

NO! Let GO of me! Please let go of me . . . !
Please let go of me.

*She holds onto the dead woman's hand and sobs. We see the Bus
Driver standing just beyond it. O.C., a SIREN wails irrelevantly,
stuck in traffic.*

EXT. BROADWAY—ACCIDENT SITE—LATER. DAY.

*There are several cop cars now, an ambulance, a police barrier, cops
everywhere, and a crowd of onlookers. Lisa is giving a statement
to DETECTIVE MITCHELL. She is completely drenched in blood. Her
clothes, boots, everything.*

*Down the street, the Bus Driver, very shaken, is giving his statement to
another detective. We can't hear what he's saying for all the honking
and street noises. But he is trying to hear what Lisa is saying, and
keeps looking at her. Lisa keeps looking at him too.*

MITCHELL

OK, Lisa? Lisa? I just want to ask you a couple
of questions, OK?

LISA

OK, sure.

MITCHELL

Now I want to ask you where you were, and
what you saw when the accident took place.
Just tell me everything you saw, even if you
think it might not be important. OK?

LISA	MITCHELL
Yes.	OK? So, where were you, on the corner? Standing by the corner? Were you in the crosswalk—?

LISA
(*On 2nd "corner"*)

No, I wasn't on the corner. I mean I was, but
I was running. I was trying to catch the bus.

MITCHELL

So, you're standing across the street. Northwest
corner.

LISA

Yes, except I wasn't standing, I was running!

LISA	MITCHELL
I was trying to catch the bus. So I happened to pass the corner, but I wasn't *standing* on the corner—	OK—Whoa whoa whoa whoa. Slow down a sec.
	So you're tryin' to catch the bus—

LISA

(Starts to cry)

Yes! Yes! I was trying to catch the bus! I was trying to catch the bus!

MITCHELL

I'm sorry Lisa, but we gotta ask you this while it's still fresh in your mind.

LISA

Could somebody call my mother?

MITCHELL

We already called your mom; but I'm gonna have 'em put another call into your mother right now, OK?

LISA

Yes. Please stop patronizing me.

MITCHELL

I'm not tryin' to patronize you. I know some of these questions might seem like they don't make a lotta sense right now—

LISA

They *do* make sense. Just *ask* me!

MITCHELL

Well, that's what I'm doin'. Now: I'm gonna ask you: From where you're standing could you see the traffic light? (*Pause*) Could you see if it

was red? Green? Yellow? Just picture it in your
mind. What color was the light?

*Lisa looks over at the Bus Driver. He is looking right at her. Lisa looks
back at Mitchell.*

> LISA
>
> I guess it was green?

> MITCHELL
>
> Green.

Lisa looks from Mitchell to the Bus Driver and back. She hesitates, then:

> LISA
>
> I think it was just an accident.

*Mitchell writes in his notebook. Lisa looks at the Bus Driver again,
who meets her eyes, then looks away to answer a question from the
other detective. Lisa keeps looking at him.*

INT. COHEN APARTMENT. DAY.

*Curtis, watching TV, looks up as Lisa passes through the room. Curtis
sees she is covered in blood.*

> CURTIS
>
> What happened to you?

> LISA
>
> Nothing: I saw a woman get her leg cut off by
> a bus.

*She goes down the hall and into her room. JOAN, her mother, 40s,
appears from the kitchen.*

JOAN

Hello?

INT. LISA'S ROOM. DAY.

The room feels small and distorted. Odd. She starts to take off her blood-soaked jacket, but her purse is over her shoulder. She drops the purse and takes off the jacket. She doesn't know what to do with it. She hangs it on the closet door.

She sits on the bed and then gets up and looks at where she sat. There's an imprint of blood on the white bedspread.

LISA

Good one, Lisa.

She starts breathing heavily. She goes into her bathroom—

INT. BATHROOM. CONTINUOUS.

She kneels down next to the toilet and opens it. She waits. She throws up into the toilet. Joan knocks on the door.

JOAN

Lisa?

LISA

Just a second . . . !

Joan comes into the bathroom.

LISA

Just a *second!*

She throws up again.

JOAN

Oh my God, what *happened* to you?!?

LISA

It's OK, Mom, it's not my blood . . . !

JOAN

What do you mean? Whose blood is it? What
happened?!

LISA

NOTHING!

*Joan kneels down and tries to help her. Lisa screams and puts her
arms around her mother and cries.*

INT. LISA'S ROOM. DAY.

*Lisa is putting on a bathrobe. Her hair and body are still matted and
streaked with blood. Joan is picking up the bloody clothes and boots.*

JOAN

I don't know if I'm going to be able to get these
clean again.

LISA

Just throw them out.

JOAN

Let me see if I can get them clean.

INT. SHOWER.

Lisa stands under the faucet, letting the water take the blood out of her hair and hands. She looks very young and little in the shower, little feet and face.

INT. KITCHEN. SIMULTANEOUS.

We hear the shower. O.C. Joan scrubs the bloody boots at the kitchen sink.

INT. KITCHEN. NIGHT.

Joan, Lisa, and Curtis eat dinner. Lisa has combed, wet hair. She is very subdued.

> JOAN
>
> Does anybody know who she was?

> LISA
>
> I don't know. I guess she lived around here. She had all these Fairway grocery bags.

> CURTIS
>
> What did they do with her leg?

> LISA
>
> I have no fucking idea.

> JOAN
>
> Hey.

INT. LISA'S ROOM. NIGHT.

Lisa is getting made up to go out. Joan knocks and comes in.

JOAN

Lisa? Are you sure you don't want me to call
in . . . ?

LISA

Oh, no thanks Mom. I mean thank you: That's
really sweet. But I'm supposed to go see Becky
anyway. I don't really want to sit here thinking
about it all night. Go to work. I'll be all right.

Joan doesn't look so sure.

EXT. MOVIE THEATER—UPPER WEST SIDE. NIGHT.

*Darren, under the marquee, sees Lisa and Becky coming toward him.
He's not happy to see Becky.*

LISA

Hey.

BECKY

Hey, Darren.

DARREN

Hey.

LISA

Did you get the tickets?

INT. MOVIE THEATER. NIGHT.

*Lisa, Darren, and Becky sit, the light from the movie flickering on
their faces. Darren is mad. Becky is enjoying their discomfiture. Lisa*

is having trouble concentrating. She gets up and walks out. Darren and Becky look at each other—not sure if she just went to the bathroom or left altogether.

INT. THEATER. NIGHT.

An upscale Off-Broadway theater. The cast is taking a curtain call. Joan, the lead, is in the middle.

INT. JOAN'S DRESSING ROOM. NIGHT.

Joan is taking her stage makeup off. There's a knock.

STAGEHAND (O.S.)

Joan? You got some flowers.

JOAN

Can you bring 'em in?

INT. THEATER LOBBY. NIGHT.

RAMON, a very well-dressed interesting-looking man, 50s, is waiting in the middle of the room. He is watching Joan across the room. She is saying good-night to some friends and admirers.

JOAN

Thank you guys so much for coming . . . ! It was really great to see you . . . !

She breaks away from them and crosses toward Ramon. He speaks with heavily Spanish-accented English—Colombian, to be specific.

JOAN

Hi—are you Ramon?

RAMON

Yes. Hello. You were wonderful—again.

JOAN

You're so sweet, thank you. And thank you for
the beautiful flowers . . . !

RAMON

You're very welcome.

JOAN

And you've seen the show before . . . ?

RAMON

Yes, two times.

JOAN

Gosh. That's very—That's a lot!

RAMON

Oh no. It's a beautiful performance.
I'm sure you will have a big success.

JOAN

Well . . . right now we're just trying to concen-
trate on what we're doing . . .

RAMON

Would you allow me to buy you a drink? There's
a nice place right down the street. Or if you
didn't eat dinner . . .

Joan sees Lisa sitting across the room, waiting.

> JOAN
>
> Oh—No—thank you. I can't. I'm just on my
> way home.

> RAMON
>
> OK, that's no problem. Tomorrow I'm going
> to London for a few days, on business, but per-
> haps when I come back . . . ?

> JOAN
>
> Um—Well—

> RAMON
>
> If it's not convenient, it's no problem.

> JOAN
>
> No no, it's OK . . . Ummmm . . . Yeah . . . !
> Sure . . . !

She laughs, embarrassed.

> RAMON
>
> OK . . .

> JOAN
>
> Um, I'm sorry, I really have to go.

> RAMON
>
> OK. That's no problem.

JOAN

Anyway, thanks again for the beautiful flowers.

RAMON

It was a privilege to meet you.

She moves away from him and goes over to Lisa. Ramon heads out.

JOAN

Hey . . . !

Lisa opens her arms and Joan hugs her.

JOAN

I thought you were at the movies . . . !

LISA

Yeah. It wasn't very good.

Joan kisses and hugs Lisa, squashing her a little. Lisa gets a little tearful. Joan squeezes her tighter.

INT. THEATER BAR/RESTAURANT. NIGHT.

Lisa is out with Joan and some of the other actors from the show. They are laughing and having a good time. Joan is having a martini.

VICTOR
(*To Joan*)

Do Shirley Temple! Shirley Temple!

Joan does an excellent Shirley Temple imitation. Everyone laughs. Lisa laughs and smiles proudly.

VICTOR

What's that one—Do the baby!

JOAN

Oh, no, that's too strange.

Everybody urges Joan on.

JOAN

OK, hold on.

She clears her throat and settles down, then does a very accurate imitation of a newborn baby crying. Everybody starts laughing, including Joan, who has to stop.

VICTOR

That is so *disturbing* . . . !

JOAN

I know: It's too weird.

LISA
(Patting her)

No it's not . . .

VICTOR

Have another drink . . . !

Everybody laughs.

JOAN

I think we can all tell I've had enough.

More laughter and chatter. Joan looks at Lisa, checking to see if this frivolity is a good idea or not. Lisa smiles at her with pride and affection. Joan smiles back lovingly.

INT. COHEN APARTMENT. DAY.

At the door, Lisa, ready for school, goes out. Joan shuts and locks the door behind her, looking fretful.

EXT. BROADWAY. DAY.

Lisa walks down the street in SLOW MOTION. She passes through a gang of boys who hassle her as she goes by.

EXT. SCHOOL. DAY.

Still in slow-motion, she arrives at school. She passes other kids, approaches the main entrance. She seems and feels completely removed from everything and everyone around her.

INT. HUMANITIES CLASS. DAY.

Lisa sits in class dully. The class is reading paperbacks of King Lear. *The teacher, JOHN, is a somewhat high-strung enthusiast.*

JOHN

Matthew, if you would read France . . . And Anthony, you read Burgundy . . .

ANTHONY

Ah. Burgundy.

JOHN

And I guess I'm gonna hog the part of Lear again . . . OK. Anthony?

John walks back and forth, play in hand. The students are all reading along. Lisa is in her own distressing world.

ANTHONY

"Most royal majesty,
I crave no more than hath your highness
Offer'd, nor will you tender less."

JOHN

"Right, noble Burgundy,
When she was dear to us, we did hold her so;
But now her price is fall'n."

INT. UPPER WEST SIDE DINER. DAY.

Lisa and Darren sit in the diner, eating club sandwiches. Two NEIGH-BORHOOD LADIES, 70s, sit in a booth nearby.

NEIGHBORHOOD LADY 1

Oh, he's wonderful: He drives all the way to see her every Saturday.

DARREN

If you didn't want to go to the movies alone with me Friday, you could have just *told* me that. You didn't need to bring Becky along as your *bodyguard.*

LISA

I didn't bring her as a bodyguard.

DARREN

Then why did you?

NEIGHBORHOOD LADY 2

That's a long drive.

NEIGHBORHOOD LADY 1

You know he has three sisters? The older ones don't speak. They haven't spoken in fourteen years

NEIGHBORHOOD LADY 2

You don't say.

NEIGHBORHOOD LADY 1

Oh, that whole family's crazy.

NEIGHBORHOOD LADY 2

Fourteen years!

NEIGHBORHOOD LADY 1

And *she* has a little dog that used to belong to the father, very ugly face. But does she love that dog. When I saw that dog I says that's the ugliest dog I ever saw. She says good! Nobody'll steal him.

NEIGHBORHOOD LADY 2

Who's gonna steal him?

NEIGHBORHOOD LADY 1

Who's gonna steal him?

LISA

I forgot I told Becky I would do something with her Friday night, so I invited her along. I didn't think it was gonna sully our whole relationship.

DARREN (*Mutters*)

What relationship?

LISA

What are you muttering?

DARREN

Nothing. I'll try to improve my diction. (*Pause*) What's the matter?

LISA

Nothing.

DARREN

Something obviously is . . .

LISA

Everything's just fucked up . . .

DARREN

Like what?

NEIGHBORHOOD LADY 1

That's what I said.

NEIGHBORHOOD LADY 2

What's the name of it?

NEIGHBORHOOD LADY 1

It's called a bull terrier.

NEIGHBORHOOD LADY 2

No, what's the name of the dog?

NEIGHBORHOOD LADY 1

Barnaby.

LISA

Just everything.

DARREN

But what specifically is fucked up?

LISA (*Very low*)

Nothing.

The two ladies keep on talking. We hear other voices, other conversations from the nearby booths and tables: A BUSINESS MAN on his cell phone, a WAITRESS and WAITER speaking in Polish, other diners, etc.

LISA
(*Low*)

So . . . I've been thinking about your suggestion . . .

DARREN

Uh huh . . . ?

LISA

I guess I don't think it's a very good idea.

DARREN

Why not?

LISA

I guess I don't feel that way about you.

DARREN

But those kinds of feelings can develop. I definitely feel like there's a connection there.

LISA
(*Very low*)

I know there is.

DARREN

I just think you're scared. I think you're scared of your own feelings. I think you've been hurt by other relationships you've had in the past, and I think what it would feel like to have a real feeling is really terrifying to you.

She wipes her eyes because tears are running down her cheeks.

DARREN

What's the matter? (*Pause*) What's the matter?

She won't look at him. O.C. AUDIENCE APPLAUSE takes us to:

INT. BAR/RESTAURANT. NIGHT.

Joan and Ramon are having a drink at a small table.

RAMON

My family are from Colombia . . . My father worked in the diplomatic service . . .

JOAN

Really. Wow.

RAMON

. . . I grew up five years in Panama, and nine years in Paris.

JOAN

And what do you do, Ramon?

RAMON

I have a company: We design computer software to help companies in South American countries that use an incompatible software, so the computers can't talk to each other. It's a big problem in Central and South America, where there is not usually so much coordination in computer communications. So right now there's a big opportunity for us, because for the big software companies it's still in the backwoods. That's changing very fast . . .

JOAN

God. Huh.

INT. RESTAURANT—COAT CHECK. NIGHT.

Joan and Ramon approach the Coat Check. Ramon gives the coat check girl their ticket.

RAMON

Can I give you a lift?

JOAN

Oh. No thank you. I'm just gonna grab a cab . . . But thanks

RAMON

May I call you sometime?

JOAN

OK, sure. That'd be great.

Silence.

RAMON

May I have your telephone number?

JOAN

Oh my God, I'm sorry, of course! Duh! Do you have a pen?

RAMON
(*Taking out his cell phone*)

What's your number?

Joan gives him her phone number.

INT. COHEN APARTMENT. NIGHT.

Joan lets herself in to the dark silent apartment.

INT. JOAN'S BEDROOM. NIGHT.

Joan lies awake, restless. She starts masturbating. After a while she kicks off the covers and hikes her nightgown up. Just as she's getting worked up there's a KNOCK on the door, and Lisa comes partway in.

LISA

Mom . . . ?

JOAN
(*Startled*)

Just a second!

LISA

Can I come in?

JOAN

Just one second, honey. Hold on! (*Covering
herself up*) Come in.

Lisa comes in and sits on the edge of the bed.

LISA

Can I talk to you?

JOAN

Sure. What's up?

Lisa hesitates.

EXT. NIGHT. FROM ACROSS THE STREET. SIMULTANEOUS.

*A slow pan across the building. We see other tenants in the windows
before we land on Lisa, talking to her mother, through Joan's little
bedroom window.*

LISA V.O.

And I guess I was *kind* of waving back, because
I was trying to get him to stop . . .

INT. JOAN'S ROOM. NIGHT. CONTINUOUS.

LISA

. . . but I'm supposed to go back to the police
to confirm my statement like the day after
tomorrow. (*Pause*) So what do you think I
should *do?*

JOAN

Well . . . it doesn't sound like it was anybody's
fault . . .

LISA

But don't you think I should say something to
them now?

JOAN

I don't know, sweetie. I mean, that bus driver
probably has a family to support . . . He
could probably lose his job . . . So I think you
should really *think* about that before you say
anything . . . You might end up feeling even
worse . . .

Lisa was not expecting this response.

LISA

OK . . .

Pause.

JOAN

OK . . . ?

KLEIN (O.C.)

Think of the implications of what you're saying!

INT. HISTORY CLASS. DAY.

ANGIE, a Syrian-American girl, has her hand up.

KLEIN

... *I'm* saying, what is the frame of reference for the average Arab on the *street*? Angie!

ANGIE

Yeah, my mother's family is from Syria? And they're not exactly in love with the current regime, and I definitely don't agree with a lot of their religious views, especially when it comes to the oppression of women. But I just want to say that Americans have *no idea* how much people hate them all over the world. OK?

BECKY

We *don't*?

ANGIE

And all my relatives in Syria think that what we did in *Afghanistan* was terrorism. Not to mention *Iraq* ...

ANTHONY

Syria is a theocratic military dictatorship.

ANGIE

Um, no it's not: Sorry.

ANTHONY

Syria is not a theocratic military dictatorship?

LISA

Um, I think we have a pretty good idea how much people hate us now actually, Angie.

ANGIE

No we *don't.*

LEWIS

One at a time—

LISA

They blew up our *city,* OK? So yeah, I think we have a pretty good idea, and personally I don't give a shit.

There is some laughter from the class.

ANGIE

You should!

LISA

—because the people who blew up the World Trade Center were a bunch of sick *monsters.*

ANGIE

Oh they were *monsters?*

LISA

Yes!

ANGIE

Why? Because they're Arabs?

LISA

No, because they killed three thousand people
for no reason.

KLEIN

Hey, hey, one at a time . . . !

ANGIE

Maybe they think they *had* a reason!

LISA

Like what? They didn't even
have any *demands!* They just
wanted to kill people!

What do you think we
should've done?

THE CLASS

They don't care about civil-
ian casualties! And Iraq has
nothing to do with Afghanistan! It has to do with oil!

LEWIS

Come on guys, one at a
time! Anthony.

KLEIN

Hey, hey, hey!

ANGIE

Why did we drop bombs
on innocent people in
Afghanistan? We're still doing
it! Why did we invade Iraq?

BECKY (*On* "we're")

Because, they declared *war*
on us, Angie!

ANGIE

No they *didn't! Iraq* didn't de-
clare war on anybody! They
didn't do anything to us!

ANTHONY

They did have a reason.

ANGIE

Thank you.

ANTHONY

They want to establish a medieval Islamic ca-
liphate in the Middle East and destroy Western
civilization.

ANGIE

Oh, where did you read that?

ANTHONY

It's on their website?

ANGIE

Okay, forget it.

KLEIN

Angie!

ANGIE

No! Forget it!

KLEIN

Go ahead with what you were saying!

ANGIE

No! Why should I?

LISA

But why are you defending somebody who murdered three thousand people?

ANGIE

I'm not! Why are *you* defending a country that unilaterally invaded two Muslim countries and supports the Israeli occupation of Palestine?!

The class ROARS—half in support and half in opposition.

LISA

Oh give me a break!

ANGIE

—and drops bombs on women and children and then calls other people terrorists for doing the exact same thing!

KLEIN	LISA
OK—OK—	Because it's not the same thing!

ANGIE

Yes it is!

KLEIN

Lionel! Go ahead.

LIONEL

Yeah, I just want to ask like, why is it OK to drop bombs on men, but it's not OK to drop

bombs on women and children? Isn't that just
reverse sexism?

KLEIN

I don't know. That's an interesting point. I
agree it's a bullshit term.

LISA

This is totally stupid.

KLEIN
(*Looking for hands*)

Uhhhhhh . . . Monica!

MONICA

Yeah, I think this whole class should apologize to Angie, because all she did was express
her opinion about what her relatives in Syria
think—

ANGIE

Thank you!

MONICA

—and everybody started screaming at her like
she was defending the Ku Klux Klan!

LISA

They *are* the Ku Klux Klan! They like to throw
acid in women's *faces!*

MONICA

Who does? The Afghanistans? Afghanies? The Iraqis?

LISA

Yes! No! The Taliban! Do you wish they were still there?

ANTHONY

The correct term is Afghans.

ANGIE

Why don't you drop bombs— Then why don't you drop bombs on the Ku Klux Klan? Because they're white?

LIONEL

There's six people with their hands raised before you, Lisa!

MONICA

(*To Lisa:*)

But I'm not even saying I disagree with you! I'm only saying I think it's pathetic the way people in this class treated Angie just for saying something they don't agree with.

KLEIN

Because that's *censorship*, right? Right?

MONICA

Yeah! (*A joke:*) Right on!

ANGIE

Thank you . . . !

ANTHONY

That's not technically true.

LISA

It's not censorship . . . ! This class is not the government!

LEWIS

It's censorship.

LISA

Oh my God, no it's not!

INT. COHEN APARTMENT. DAY.

Lisa is sitting in the living room, ready to go out. Joan enters, coat on, purse in hand.

> JOAN

Ready?

EXT. LOCAL POLICE PRECINCT. DAY.

Joan and Lisa walk down 83rd Street past brownstones and green trees until they arrive at the police station. They go in.

INT. LOCAL POLICE PRECINCT—INTERVIEW ROOM. DAY.

Mitchell walks Joan and Lisa into the interview room.

> MITCHELL

We actually work outta Highway One? Up in the Bronx? Near the Bronx Zoo? So for somethin' like this we just borrow a local precinct . . .

> JOAN

Uh huh . . .

INT. INTERVIEW ROOM. DAY—LATER.

Lisa and Joan sit with Mitchell. He writes down Lisa's answers.

> MITCHELL

According to your statement the light was green when the bus went through the intersection?

> LISA

Yes.

MITCHELL

So you're sayin' she walked against the light.

Pause. Lisa glances at Joan. Joan smiles at her encouragingly. Lisa turns to Mitchell. Starts to speak—

INT. THEATER. NIGHT.

Joan is onstage with fellow actor Victor. Lisa sits in the audience.

JOAN

It's true. Two years of college. Two years at the magazine. Two years with you. (*Bursts into tears*) I'm kind of a two-year gal . . . !

The audience laughs. Lisa watches, unamused.

INT. CAB (MOVING) NIGHT.

Joan and Lisa sit in the rattling cab. There is a long and deliberate silence.

JOAN

What did you think of the play?

LISA

It was OK.

Silence.

JOAN

Well, thank you, honey.

EXT. SANTA MONICA—KARL'S HOUSE. DAY.

WIDE: A shabby bungalow house on the beach, off Route 1 in Santa Monica. The phone is ringing inside.

INT. KARL'S HOUSE. DAY./INT. COHEN APARTMENT. NIGHT.

KARL, 45, answers. He is a displaced New Yorker who has never quite settled down. WE CUT BETWEEN THEM.

                    KARL
        Hello?

                    LISA
        Hi Dad!

                    KARL
        Yeah! Hi!

                    LISA
        How are you?

                    KARL
        I'm great. I'm looking at a beautiful sunset over
        the ocean. Doing a little work . . . How are you?

                    LISA
        I'm OK.

                    KARL
        Practicing your horseback riding?

LISA
(*Laughs*)

Oh yeah, I'm really riding a lot. I'm getting these really bad saddle sores.

KARL

OK. Well. I would actually seriously recommend you go over to, uh, to Claremont Stables over on 89th Street and see about getting some lessons.

LISA

No, I was actually really thinking about doing that . . .

KARL

So how's everything going? How's school?

LISA

School's OK. I'm kind of fucking up in geometry . . .

KARL

I assume you're not topedoeing your scholarship, or anything like that?

LISA

Nope—scholarship's fine.

KARL

OK good. Well, math was never my strong suit either.

LISA

Well, I am definitely following in your footsteps in that regard . . .

KARL

Well, I'm proud to hear it.

Lisa laughs.

LISA

So how are you?

KARL

I'm fine. I'm good. Things are OK. They're a little slow . . . A little—frustrating. But there are one or two projects we're going after that seem to look promising . . . Which is good. And . . . I don't know. Um . . . How's the boyfriend situation?

LISA

Oh the same. They're all kind of the same.

KARL

No fascinating young men knocking at your door?

LISA

Yeah, very few fascinating young men at my school.

KARL

Well, I know this is not going to go anywhere, but Annette's workshop is comprised for the most part of strapping young men of about seventeen years old who for some peculiar reason are interested in using their brains to get on with their lives. Nobody understands why or how this happened, but if you're interested in meeting any of them when you come out next time—

LISA

Yeah, I mean, I don't really go for the California type.

Pause.

KARL

Well—I don't either, per se. It somewhat depends on who it is, obviously . . .

LISA

Hard to argue with. I think I'll stop generalizing now . . . !

KARL

OK. Well, that's about all on my end, babe. I'll give you a call in a week or two. Give my love to Curtis, and say hello to your mom.

LISA

OK, I can't wait for our trip.

KARL

Yeah. I think we're gonna have a really good
time.

LISA	KARL
OK. Well, I love you.	. . . It's gonna be really fun. Um—Love you too.

LISA

Bye Dad.

KARL

Bye sweetie.

EXT. KARL'S HOUSE. DAY.

*Karl steps onto his deck. We hear the Santa Monica Route 1 traffic
O.C.*

INT. LISA'S ROOM—LATER.

Lisa lies on the bed next to the hung-up phone.

INT. STUDENT LOUNGE—OUTSIDE THE THEATER OFFICE. DAY.

*PAUL, a droll, handsome senior, is holding court, feet up on a desk,
an unlit cigarette in his hand.*

PAUL

Yeah, like I would be in a movie, only I would
be doing exactly what I'm doing right now:
Like I'd be sitting here smoking a cigarette,
and I'd have my feet up on the desk, but the

camera would be on me and I'd just be acting, except I wouldn't do anything differently from how I'm doing it right now.

Nearby, Becky and Lisa are looking at a school poster for The Pirates Of Penzance.

BECKY

I can't believe you didn't audition for *Pirates of Penzance.* You're such a good singer.

LISA

I still might do lights or something. But I'm not gonna make a fuckin' ass out of myself parading around in a play so I can ask everyone how great I was for three years afterwards like my fuck-ass mother.

Lisa looks over toward Paul.

INT. FANCY RESTAURANT. NIGHT.

Joan is at a table with Ramon in a very expensive restaurant.

JOAN

You do know I have two kids, right?

RAMON

Yes. I'd like to meet them.

JOAN

You are really smooth.

RAMON

I would love to meet your kids. I have two boys
myself. I'm not smooth. (*Pause*) Would you like
to have a nightcap?

JOAN

Oh, God.

INT. BECKY'S ROOM. NIGHT.

Becky and Lisa are smoking pot. They are dolled up.

BECKY

Are you aware that things have gotten to the
point where I now have to hear things about
you from other people and I can't even correct
them because I no longer have any first-hand
information about you myself?

LISA

What are you talking about?

BECKY

Nothing. I just feel like we used to be really
close—like, up until a few days ago. And I'm
not really getting that from you anymore.

LISA

Becky. Give me a break.

Pause.

BECKY

I can't believe you just said that to me. That was really hard for me to say, and *that's* your response?

LISA

Can we just go please?

BECKY

Fine. Would you like to smoke any more of my pot before we leave or have you had as much as you want now?

LISA
(*Sarcastic back*)

Oh, I'd like to have a little bit more please.

BECKY

Fine. Get fuckin' out of my house!

LISA

Fine. But this is totally stupid because we're both going to the same party.

INT. PARTY HOUSE—BATHROOM. NIGHT.

The door opens and we catch a glimpse of a big party in a brownstone full of circulating kids. Lisa and Paul cram into the bathroom and shut the door again.

A MOMENT LATER—She is sitting on the toilet. He is on the hamper, opening a small vial of coke.

LISA

It's very hard to be cool under these circumstances.

PAUL

You don't have to be cool. All you have to do is snort it up your nose.

LISA

I'll try . . . !

He gives her the spoon. She snorts it.

PAUL

And then you wanna do the other nostril because you always want to be symmetrical. Very important.

She snorts some up the other nostril. Paul does some too and closes the vial.

PAUL

Symmetry.

LISA

You are so funny . . . ! (*Pause*) So what do we do now?

PAUL

Now we make out.

LISA

Paul . . . ! What about your girlfriend?

Pause.

PAUL

I'm sorry. It just sounded like you just asked me about my girlfriend.

LISA

Oh, never mind . . .

They make out. He immediately starts feeling her up. She pushes his hand away.

PAUL

You're not serious.

LISA

Oh . . . No.

He moves his hand back. She lets him.

INT. PARTY HOUSE—STAIRWELL. NIGHT.

Lisa comes down around the stairs at a mellow stoned and drunken pace. She sees Darren sitting by himself on the floor at the end of a hallway. She walks over to him and slowly sits down next to him.

LISA

Hey . . . You know I really love you, right?

DARREN

Not really.

Pause. She kisses him softly and they make out for a minute.

LISA

I guess I'm not very consistent.

DARREN

I don't mind.

She kisses him again. She draws back slightly.

LISA

I gotta go home.

DARREN

OK . . .

INT. RAMON'S BATHROOM. NIGHT.

Joan stands by the sink, naked, smoking, a little overexcited. Ramon KNOCKS. She jumps.

RAMON (O.C.)

Joan? Are you all right?

JOAN

Yes! Fine! Be out in a sec.

She gets up, flushes the cigarette, looks in the mirror, tousles her hair, snaps off the light, and opens the door.

INT. SCHOOL—GYMNASIUM. DAY.

Lisa and her coed class watch BONNIE, a young tall beautiful no-makeup gymnastics teacher.

BONNIE

OK, so we're just gonna start with a couple of
simple stretches. So just watch me first, and
then you'll follow.

She stretches. Lisa notices the boys looking at Bonnie.

INT. GEOMETRY CLASS. DAY.

The last students file out except Lisa. Mr. Aaron is erasing the blackboard.

LISA

Mr. Aaron?

MR. AARON

Yes, Becky? Um—Lisa?

LISA

Are you still mad at me about the test?

MR. AARON

What's going on, Lisa?

INT. GEOMETRY CLASS—A FEW MINUTES LATER. DAY.

Lisa and Mr. Aaron sit at his desk.

LISA

. . . Because maybe my mother is right, and the
bus driver is completely devastated as it is. And
I'm just gonna be this little rich girl who calls
up the cops to ease her conscience, and then
ends up ruining somebody's life, when I'm the
one who was distracting him in the first place.

MR. AARON

What does your being rich have to do with anything?

LISA

You know what I mean.

MR. AARON

No, I don't.

LISA

Oh my God, I don't mean *literally* rich. I mean rich compared to the bus driver.

MR. AARON

I still don't see what that has to do with whether you tell the police the truth or not about the accident you witnessed.

Lionel opens the classroom door.

MR. AARON

Lionel? It's gonna be five minutes.

LIONEL

I just thought you'd want to know there's like, a lot of people out here, and it's getting kind of hard to breathe.

MR. AARON

You better close that door *now,* Lionel.

Lionel closes the door.

MR. AARON

All right. Um . . . I have to let those guys in. I
don't want to leave you hangin' . . . If you're
really hurtin' . . . we could get a cup of coffee
after school . . .

LISA

I'd do that.

Mr. Aaron sighs a little.

EXT. COFFEE SHOP. DAY.

*Through a window we see Mr. Aaron and Lisa talking. A variety of
pedestrians pass by the coffee shop.*

INT. LIVING ROOM. NIGHT.

Lisa is watching TV. Joan comes in dressed for the opera.

JOAN

Hey. Does this dress make me look fat?

LISA

Um, a little.

JOAN

Well, there's nothing I can do about it.

LISA

Where are you going?

JOAN

The opera . . . !

LISA

Why are you going to the *opera?*

JOAN

It turns out he's a really big opera fan . . . !
Anyway, don't you think it's kind of fun? We
should all go sometime.

LISA

Uh, no thanks.

JOAN

Why not? I bet you'd like it.

LISA

I don't like that kind of singing.

JOAN

But you like classical music.

LISA

Yes. That's true. But I don't like opera singing.

JOAN

But when have you ever—

LISA

It's like their entire reason
for existing is to prove how
loud they can be. I don't
really find that all that
interesting.

JOAN

Yeah. I know what you mean. But it's not *all*
like that. You like *The Magic Flute.*

LISA

OK. I guess I'm wrong. I guess I *do* like opera singing. I just didn't realize it.

Pause.

JOAN

What is the matter with you?

LISA

Nothing at all! Why are you pushing this? I don't want to go to the opera!

JOAN

Yes! OK! It's called an *invitation.* I'm not pushing anything! All you have say is "No thanks!"

LISA

I did! And then you were like, "Why not?" So then I *told* you, and then you started like, *debating* me! Like you assume I've never thought this through for myself! Which I have! Many times!

JOAN

OK, well, that was a really contemptuous assumption on my part. I don't actually like the opera that much myself. But I'm trying to expand my mind. Maybe that's wrong! (*Pause*) I'm sorry. I guess I'm a little nervous about you guys meeting Ramon.

LISA

Why? What's the big deal? Why are you so in-
fluenced by what me and Curtis think? What
Curtis and *I* think.

JOAN

Because obviously if I'm seeing somebody new
it would important to me that you guys would
like him and that he like you. Why wouldn't I
be nervous about that?

LISA

I guess you would. Withdrawn.

JOAN

Hey, why does everything I say annoy you?

LISA

Jesus Christ, I'm just *sitting* here!

JOAN

Here: You be me, and say anything, and I'll
respond the way you've been responding to
me this whole conversation.

LISA

No . . . !

JOAN

Go ahead: Say something to
me and I'll say something to
you the way you say everything
to me—Why not?

LISA

No! I'm not gonna do that.

LISA

Because it's dumb! I'm horrible! I get your point!

JOAN
(*Like Lisa*)

"OK, uh, whatever."

LISA

Was that supposed to be an imitation of me?

JOAN

"Um, OK: *Withdrawn.*"

Lisa shakes her head and watches the TV. Pause.

JOAN

Are you coming to my opening night?

LISA

I will if I have to.

Pause.

JOAN

You're a little cunt, do you know that?

LISA

Yes. You're a big cunt.

JOAN

OK. Let's not start talking to each other that way.

LISA

You just called me a cunt, Mom!

JOAN

OK, I'm sorry I said that.   LISA
But if you're really saying—   Why? It's refreshing!

JOAN

—If you're really saying you're not aware that
you've been really annoyed with me, or really
irritable with me—and it doesn't matter if I
express it exactly accurately: You know what
I'm trying to say—!

LISA

Not really.

JOAN

If you're saying you're completely unaware of
that, then I have to say I don't think you're
being honest about it. Now maybe I'm doing
something really horrible to you without being
aware of it, but I have a show opening in two
weeks, I'm very nervous about it, I'm seeing a
new person and I'm obviously anxious about
you and Curtis liking him—whether you think I
should be or not!—you were involved in a horrible traumatic accident, you're going on this
crazy horseback riding trip with your father—

LISA

Oh my *God!*

JOAN

—which sounds like a recipe for *disaster* to me!
And on top of everything else, Lisa, ever since
I told you about Ramon you've been treating
me like I'm *insane!*

LISA

Um, I think you're exaggerating slightly.

JOAN

Now what am I supposed to do?!

LISA

Just—

JOAN

What am I supposed to do?!

LISA

Just stop *whining* about everything! It doesn't
matter. None of that matters at *all!* You've been
in a million plays, you always get freaked out
because of what some dumb critic is gonna
say about your dumb play, I don't frankly give
a shit about Ramon or *who* you're going out
with this week—

JOAN

I never go out with anyone!
Don't *talk* to me that way!
I've barely had a *date* in the
last two years!

LISA

Right! I don't care!

LISA

But I don't care about *any* of this! It doesn't matter! Your boyfriend doesn't matter! Your play doesn't matter, except to you! I don't care about New Mexico, because to tell you the truth I'm probably not even *going*—

JOAN

What do you mean?

LISA

—and you want to know something else, Mom? There are more important problems in the world than our *relationship!* There's a whole city out there full of people who are *dying!* So who cares if I like your fucking *boyfriend?* It's so *trivial!* Why are you bothering me about all this? It doesn't *matter!*!!

Pause. The intercom buzzes. Joan hesitates.

JOAN

Well—should I have him come up now? Or should I have him wait downstairs . . . ?

LISA

Do whatever you want. *I don't care!*

JOAN

Lisa, I don't even know what we're talking about.

LISA

I know you don't. That's the problem.

JOAN

Oh give me a break.

EXT. LINCOLN CENTER. NIGHT.

Ramon and Joan walk toward the Metropolitan Opera House.

RAMON

Everything is all right?

JOAN

Oh, yeah. I'm so excited to be going to the *opera!* I don't think I've really gone more than one or two times!

RAMON

Well, I wish it wasn't *Norma.* But still, it's fun to go.

JOAN
(*A joke:*)

What if we just went to see something else instead?

RAMON

You don't want to hear *Norma?*

JOAN

No—I don't mean that. I just meant wouldn't it be funny if we just walked into one of the

other events? Like if we just went to see the
Daniel Goldfarb play instead?

RAMON

You don't want to hear Norma?

JOAN

No no, it's not that—

INT. METROPOLITAN OPERA. NIGHT.

Joan and Ramon sit in the audience listening to Norma. *Joan leans
in toward Ramon and whispers:*

JOAN

It's beautiful . . . !

RAMON

Shhh.

INT. LISA'S ROOM/PAUL'S ROOM. NIGHT.

*Lisa dials a phone number off a 11th grade class contact sheet. The
line rings. WE CUT BETWEEN THEM.*

PAUL
(*Answering the phone*)

Yo.

LISA

Hey, Paul.

PAUL

Hey.

LISA

It's Lisa Cohen.

PAUL

Yeah, how's it going?

LISA

OK. (*Pause*) What have you been up to?

PAUL

Seeing some questionable movies. Not decid-
ing where to go to college . . .

LISA

Sounds good . . . (*Pause*) So . . . I was just
thinking . . . This is gonna sound really queer,
but . . . by any chance would you want to meet
somewhere and like, take away my virginity?

PAUL

Um . . . all right.

LISA

Really? God, I'm so flattered.

PAUL

To what do I owe this inconceivable honor?

LISA

Actually, it's because of my deep passionate
feelings for you, Paul.

PAUL

That's pretty much what I figured . . . (*Pause*)
So, do you want to come over here? Should I
come over there . . . ?

LISA

Well, my mom just went out for the evening . . .

PAUL

All right. (*Pause*) Do you want to give me your
address?

LISA
(*Blushing almost to death*)

It's 252 West 85th Street . . .

INT. DARREN'S ROOM/LISA'S ROOM. NIGHT.

*Darren lies on his bed, depressed. He sits at his computer and checks
his email. Nothing. He dials the phone.*

LISA
(*On the phone*)

Hello?

DARREN

Hey. What are you up to?

LISA

Hey, nothing. Writing my *King Lear* paper.

DARREN

Really? That's impressive.

LISA

Not really.

DARREN

I've just never known you to be so devoted to your studies before.

LISA

Well, I don't want to fail Humanities.

DARREN

You're not gonna fail Humanities.

LISA

No, probably not.

DARREN

So what did you do tonight?

LISA

Actually, Darren . . . I don't really feel like talking right now.

Pause.

DARREN

OK.

LISA

OK?

DARREN

Yeah. I'll talk to you later.

> LISA

OK.

> DARREN

OK, bye.

> LISA

Bye.

Darren hangs up and starts crying.

INT. LISA'S ROOM. SIMULTANEOUS.

Lisa hangs up slowly. She moves to the mirror and looks at herself.

INT. HALL. NIGHT.

Lisa, dressed up and wearing some makeup, opens the door for Paul. He's not dressed up at all. He's smoking.

> PAUL

Hey.

> LISA

Hey, come in.

She steps aside. He passes her and comes in.

> PAUL

I think I just alienated one of your neighbors
by smoking in the elevator.

> LISA

Oh really? What did they say?

PAUL

She basically said there was no smoking in the
elevator.

LISA

That's original . . .

TRACKING them as they come into the living room . . .

LISA

So this is the living room.

PAUL

Very livable.

LISA

We like it . . . My mom hasn't read any of these
books, by the way.

PAUL

Have you?

LISA

Some of them. Not all of them.

Paul picks up and looks at The Rise and Fall of the Third Reich.

PAUL

This book is a very cool book.

LISA

Yeah, I think the Third Reich may be a little
bit too much for me right now.

> PAUL

It's pretty hard to put down once you get started.

> LISA

Do you want anything to drink?

> PAUL

I'd take a beer.

INT. KITCHEN. NIGHT.

Lisa has two beers out and is looking through drawers.

> LISA

OK, I have no idea where the bottle opener is.

> PAUL

Here, lemme have them.

He takes the beers and opens them on the edge of the counter. He makes two marks in the counter doing this.

> LISA

Thanks.

> PAUL

Whoops. I think I just permanently damaged your kitchen counter. Sorry.

> LISA

Oh—that's OK. Don't worry about it.

PAUL

Won't your Mother be Upset?

LISA

How come everything you say always sounds so ironic? You don't even have to *do* anything and it just comes out sounding like, totally ironic and funny.

PAUL

It's just a gift.

She laughs nervously. They drink beer.

LISA

So . . . do you want to see my room?

PAUL

Sure.

INT. LISA'S ROOM. NIGHT.

They come into her room. She closes the door.

LISA

This is my room. Ta da.

PAUL

Very nice.

She realizes she has some stuffed animals on the bed.

LISA

And these are my stuffed animals.

PAUL

Always important to meet the stuffed animals.

LISA

These are some drawings I did . . . Not that I should be showing them to *you*, because I know you're like a really good artist, right?

PAUL

I would *like* to be a really good artist. At this point I think it would be more accurate to say I'm good at drawing.

LISA

Yeah, I just do it for fun. But I've always really liked it . . .

He looks at her pictures.

LISA

So . . . can I ask you a question?

PAUL

Yes?

LISA

This is probably gonna sound very immature, but how can you be so relaxed, knowing what we're about to do? Or is it just like no big deal to you? (*Pause*) OK, that was a really stupid question and I'm like totally embarrassed right now. I'm actually more embarrassed than I've ever been in my life. If you want to go home now that's totally OK.

PAUL

Easy there. Don't be embarrassed. It's basically like, the world's greatest activity, but it's not actually worth getting nervous about.

LISA

Yeah: I don't usually get nervous because I think it's worth it: I usually get nervous because I can't help the way I feel.

PAUL

There is that philosophy.

LISA

You are so funny . . . !

PAUL

Do you have an ashtray?

LISA

Oh, you can just chuck it out the window.

Paul struggles to open the window and tosses his cigarette. He closes the window and comes across the room to kiss her.

LISA

Are we starting?

PAUL

I was thinking about it, yeah.

LISA

I'm sorry. I guess I'm a little nervous. Please
ignore.

PAUL

Don't be nervous. I promise, this is gonna be
a great experience for you.

He kisses her. They make out.

PAUL

OK, let's talk about your kissing.

Lisa collapses with her face in the bed.

PAUL

Don't panic. It's just a technical thing.

LISA

What are you, like, the nicest guy in the world?

PAUL

No . . .

INT. LISA'S ROOM. NIGHT. LATER.

*It's dark. Their clothes are off, but we don't see much. She is giving
him a handjob.*

LISA

Like that?

PAUL
(*Not quite, but close enough*)

Yes . . .

LISA

Am I supposed to go really fast at the end or
something?

PAUL

Yeah, but we're gonna move on before
that . . . Here:

He shifts around and tries to go down on her.

LISA

You don't have to do that.

PAUL

I know. I want to.

Pause. She slides up away from him.

LISA

Don't do that, OK? I'm just embarrassed. Let
me do it to you.

PAUL

All right.

INT. LISA'S ROOM. LATER.

He is positioning himself on top of her.

PAUL

Are you ready?

LISA

Yeah.

PAUL

OK. This is a little tricky: It's probably gonna hurt a little, at first, but then it's gonna get better . . . Just be patient. There are certain technical difficulties on my end that have to be addressed or it's not gonna happen.

LISA

OK: You sound insane.

They laugh.

PAUL

OK, ready?

LISA
(*Suddenly frightened*)

Yeah.

PAUL

OK?

LISA
(*In some pain*)

Mm hm.

PAUL

OK, hang on . . .

LISA

Ow . . . !

PAUL

OK—There we go. Does it hurt now?

LISA

Kind of, yeah.

PAUL

OK, just try to relax. It'll get better in a second . . .

LISA

Did you bring a condom?

PAUL

Uh huh . . .

LISA

Shouldn't you put it on?

PAUL

I will in a second.

LISA

This is really kind of hurting.

PAUL

OK—one second.

                    LISA

I love you.

                    PAUL

What?

                    LISA

Nothing.

                    PAUL

OK—hold on—Shit—

                    LISA

What?

                    PAUL

OK, one second—Ohh! Sorry—Sorry—

He comes inside her. Silence. He carefully rolls over.

                    PAUL

Sorry about that. Kind of got away from me.

                    LISA

Did any of it get inside me?

                    PAUL

I don't know.

                    LISA
                 (*Feeling around*)

Yeah. It definitely did.

PAUL

Honest to God? It's probably OK. The odds
are overwhelmingly that it's OK.

O.C. the doorbell rings.

LISA

That's my little brother.

*She gets a bathrobe and goes out. We TRACK HER through the whole
apartment. She opens the door for Curtis.*

LISA

Hi, Curtis.

CURTIS

Hi.

*We TRACK her back to her room. She shuts the door. Paul has put on
his underwear and is smoking a cigarette.*

PAUL

Hey.

LISA

Hey. (*Sits down*) Can I have a drag? (*Takes a drag
of his cigarette*) Thanks. (*Gives it back to him*) I'm
actually kind of mad at you . . .

PAUL

Why? (*Pause*) Why? (*Pause*) Because we didn't
use birth control?

LISA

I guess so.

PAUL

It was at the *ready* . . .

LISA

Well, I don't really want to get AIDS, you know? And I really don't want to have an abortion, because I know when you have one at my age it can be really hard to get pregnant later on, and I definitely want to have children someday.

PAUL

Try to listen to me. Right about now is when you're traditionally supposed to freak out. So why don't you just *not?* You're not gonna get AIDS, because I don't have AIDS—

LISA

How do you know? Have you been tested?

PAUL

No, but I'm pretty sure I don't have it, because of my demographic. And the odds are you're probably not gonna have to have an abortion either. And since this was your first time, it might as well be a basically happy memory instead of a shitty one.

LISA

I'm sorry. I'm not completely in control of my emotions. (*Pause*) Anyway . . . Thank you for deflowering me.

PAUL

You're welcome.

LISA

Did it freak you out that I said I love you?

PAUL

No . . . It didn't freak me out.

LISA

You don't have to say it back, because I know you probably have like, no feelings at all for me.

PAUL

I think I just proved I have *some* feelings for you.

LISA

You should probably go now . . .

Paul starts to get dressed. Lisa waits.

INT. LISA'S ROOM. NIGHT.

She changes into her pajamas.

LISA'S BATHROOM. NIGHT.

She washes her face and brushes her teeth.

INT. LIVING ROOM. NIGHT.

She comes out and settles down next to Curtis to watch TV.

INT. METROPOLITAN OPERA. NIGHT.

The audience applauds the opera cast thunderously. Near Joan and Ramon, a male opera enthusiast is standing.

> OPERA FAN

Bravi! Bravi!

EXT. LINCOLN CENTER. NIGHT.

Joan and Ramon walk arm in arm away from Lincoln Center.

> JOAN

Oh, I loved it! It was so exciting. But how about those people yelling "Bravi!" and "Brava!"

> RAMON

How do you mean?

> JOAN

It's just so pretentious. "Bravi! Bravi!" Why can't they just say "Bravo?"

> RAMON

Well, it's the plural.

> JOAN

I know—

> RAMON

It's what they say to acknowledge the ensemble.

JOAN

No, I know, I know it's correct, it just—don't you think there was something a little pretentious about those people?

RAMON

Pretentious?

JOAN

I don't mean they didn't really enjoy it . . . But you know how you can really be enjoying something—but you're also kind of looking around out of the corner of your eye—because you know people are watching you enjoy it . . . ? Does that make sense at all?

RAMON

Yes, but I wouldn't say that it was pretentious. In Italian you say "Bravo" for the man and "Brava" for the woman, and "Bravi" for the whole company.

JOAN

Uh huh? OK, I see what you mean.

RAMON

You use the masculine for the male singer and the feminine for the female singer.

JOAN

Yeah . . . Anyway, I really enjoyed it. Thank you.

RAMON

We'll have to go again.

JOAN

It was so glamorous . . . !

INT. SCHOOL THEATER—LIGHTING BOOTH. DAY.

Lisa is manning the lighting booth. She wears a headset. Below on the stage, Matthew is singing.

MATTHEW
(*Sings*)

"O, men of dark and dismal fate—"

LISA
(*Into headset*)

Cue thirty-six, go.

GARY THE THEATER TEACHER (O.C.)

OK, hold up a second.

LISA
(*Into headset*)

OK, we're gonna do that one more time please.
Let's back it up please . . .

INT. SCHOOL THEATER. NIGHT.

All the kids in the show are sitting more or less in a circle. GARY the theater teacher, 40s, has the floor.

GARY

Now I know there's been a lot of shit going on
between a lot of the people in this room. But I
wanna tell you something: You've worked too
fucking hard for this show to be derailed now
by the kind of bullshit I know has been going
on around here. Now, I'll bet you there's not
one person working on this show who hasn't
got somebody they want to say something to,
including me. So I'm gonna start. Matthew?

MATTHEW
(*Slowly*)
By "Matthew," I assume you mean me?

GARY

Yes. I mean you.

Matthew comes slowly into the middle of the circle.

MATTHEW

Yes?

GARY

You are probably one of the most talented kids
who's ever performed at this school. But you're
too Goddamn lazy, you think you can just waltz
through this part, and it's pissing me off. Because this show cannot come together until
you learn your fucking lines. OK?

MATTHEW

So you'd like me to memorize them.

Everyone laughs.

GARY

Yes, I'd like you to memorize them.

Everyone laughs.

INT. SCHOOL THEATER. NIGHT. LATER.

Becky and Lisa are in the circle, both crying.

BECKY

And it's like, I was so jealous of you that I wasn't even there for you when that whole thing happened with that woman . . . !

LISA

But *I'm* jealous of *you* . . . !

BECKY

Why would you be jealous of *me* . . . ?

LISA

Because of everything! 'Cause your family never has to worry about money, and your parents are still together, and I'm really jealous of your other friends!

BECKY

Well, I'm really sorry if I hurt you!

LISA

Me too!

They embrace tearfully. Many of the kids are moved. Some are not. Becky leaves Lisa in the circle. Lisa wipes her eyes.

LISA

Darren . . . ?

Darren unglues himself from his perch on a table, and sits in the circle with her.

LISA

I know that I'm not who you want me to be to you. And I know how much I've hurt you. But I still can't believe it means we can't be friends anymore! So much has been happening to me this semester—

DARREN
(*With empathy*)

I know . . . I know . . .

LISA
(*In tears*)

—and it's like I can't even talk to you about it because I hurt you so bad!

DARREN

Yes you can. Of course you can. You can talk to me about anything.

LISA

I don't love anybody more than you! You're practically my best friend!

DARREN

I love you too. I really do . . . !

They hug and cry. Leslie raises her hand.

GARY

Leslie?

LESLIE

Can I just say, I think this show is like two and a half seconds away from being fucking amazing, and if we could all just work *together,* instead of being AT each other all the time, I think we could all just be incredible.

Everyone applauds, except Angie, who raises her hand.

GARY

Angie.

ANGIE

Yeah. (*Long pause*) Yeah. I'm gonna say it. I feel really fucked over by some of the people in this room. I'm not saying I'm not gonna do my job, but for some reason, a lot of the actors in this show seem to think that this whole show is about *them.* And I think I speak for a lot of the techies when I say that I feel really unappreciated and basically fucked over. And I don't know if I can get over it. I don't. That's all.

Nobody says anything. Paul raises a hand. His pretty GIRLFRIEND is seated next to him.

GARY

Yes, Paul?

PAUL

Yeah, I'm just playing in the *band,* you know? This is *high* school. You know? I don't really feel a strong need to like, all be on the same *team* with everybody. I just want to come to rehearsals, do the show, go up on the roof and smoke some pot, and then like, go on *home.* I don't really wanna cry and hug anybody.

There are laughs and some cheers.

GARY

Oh, you wanna hug me a little, don't you Paul?

PAUL

OK, Gary, man, I'll give you a little hug. No kissin' though.

Gary charges over and hugs Paul. Everyone laughs and claps. Gary grabs Paul's face and kisses him on the cheek. Everyone is laughing.

Lisa looks at Paul, who settles back with his girlfriend. He sees Lisa looking at him and gives her a little salute. Lisa catches Darren's eye. He is looking at her with the unwelcome gaze of love. She looks away. His heart hardens against her. Becky looks at Lisa, but Lisa is very far away.

INT. COHEN APARTMENT. LIVING ROOM./INT. HIGHWAY ONE POLICE STATION. DAY.

Lisa is on the phone. Curtis is watching TV.

> MITCHELL
> (*On phone*)

Accident Investigation. Detective Mitchell.

> LISA

Hi, my name is Lisa Cohen. I was a witness in a bus accident case a few weeks ago . . .

> MITCHELL

Yeah, hi, Lisa, what can I do for you?

> LISA

Well, this is probably gonna sound a little weird, but are you allowed to tell me how to get in touch with that woman's family? I really wanted to send some flowers or something . . .

> MITCHELL

Yeah, I can—

> LISA

. . . or is that like classified information?

> MITCHELL

No no. Family's been notified . . . Lemme see what I got.

> LISA

She mentioned she had a daughter . . .

MITCHELL

Lemme just . . . OK: I don't have anything for
a daughter. The only contact I have is a cousin,
Abigail Berwitz. I got a number in Arizona . . .

LISA

So did you have the trial, or whatever? Or did
you make the—did they have a ruling yet?

MITCHELL

Yes. It was, uh, No Criminality found. OK?

LISA

No Criminality.

MITCHELL

Right.

LISA

Wow. That's a—great system you got. OK. Wow.

MITCHELL

OK?

LISA

Yeah.

INT. LISA'S ROOM. DAY.

Lisa is on the phone. We hear ABIGAIL over the phone but don't see her.

LISA

Yes, I'm trying to reach Abigail Berwitz?

ABIGAIL

This is Abigail.

LISA

Hi, my name is Lisa Cohen. You don't know
me . . . I . . .

ABIGAIL

Yes? Hello?

LISA

Hi. Sorry. Yeah. I was actually calling about your
cousin, Monica Patterson?

ABIGAIL

OK . . . ?

LISA

I was actually there when she had—during the
accident. I didn't know her, but I was the one
who was with her when she died . . .

ABIGAIL

OK . . . ?

LISA

Yeah. I was sort of holding her hand at the
time . . .

ABIGAIL

Yes? What can I do for you?

LISA

OK. Well, ummm, I saw her obituary in the paper, but I didn't see anything about a funeral. I assume they had one, because—

ABIGAIL
(*On "assume"*)

No. As far as I know they're doing something or other next week. But—

LISA

I'm sorry: And I was also wondering, she said something about her daughter?

ABIGAIL

No. Her daughter—No—
Her's daughter's not alive
—She passed away quite a
a long time ago.

LISA

She wanted someone to get
ahold of her?—I'm sorry.

LISA

Oh my God. Was it . . . Was she sick? Or was it—

ABIGAIL

She had leukemia?

LISA

Oh my gosh. And—do you mind if I ask: Was her name Lisa?

ABIGAIL

Yes . . . ?

LISA

OK, see, that explains it. See, I think she thought—

ABIGAIL

Could I just interrupt? How did you get this number?

LISA

Oh—the police—I asked the Accident Investigating investigator who to contact if I wanted to—

ABIGAIL
(*On "if"*)

Well they really shouldn't be giving out my number. This is *harassment!*

LISA
(*Shocked*)

I'm sorry! I'm not trying to harass you—!

ABIGAIL

I have been getting calls about this for three weeks! One of Monica's neighbors gave the police my number and all of a sudden I am the focal point for all these *arrangements!* And I gotta tell you people, I didn't have any kind of relationship with Monica whatsoever, unless you want to count the fact that she held up my children's inheritance for fifteen years. I guess we're just supposed to forget about all that now. And I am more than willing. But the

person you should be calling is Emily Morrison,
who was Monica's friend and is the person who
has been dealing with all of this in New York.
But it has nothing to do with me.

                    LISA

I'm sorry! I didn't really know who to contact—

                   ABIGAIL

Now I can give you her number, but I would
very much appreciate it if the calls would stop.

                    LISA

Yes—Please. Can you hold on while I get a pen?

                   ABIGAIL

Yes, all right.

INT. EMILY'S CENTRAL PARK WEST APARTMENT. DAY.

*EMILY MORRISON, early 50s, opens the door for LISA. In the b.g., about
thirty people are gathered. A mix of Upper West Siders, social workers,
and Monica's multi-ethnic clients.*

                   EMILY

Hi. Are you Lisa?

                    LISA

Yeah. Thank you so much for letting me come.

                   EMILY

Why don't you come on in? We're about to
start. Do you want anything to drink?

LISA

Oh—Um—no thanks.

EMILY

We have bad hors d'oeuvres and good hors
d'oeuvres.

LISA

Oh—that's quite all right, thank you.

INT. EMILY'S LIVING ROOM. DAY.

Everyone is seated on Emily's chairs and borrowed chairs.

EMILY

Well . . . thank you all for coming.

WOMAN MOURNER

Thank you for doing this, Emily.

THE MOURNERS

Yes, thank you, Emily.

EMILY

As you all know, Monica was not a religious
woman. Anybody who ever had to sit through
a wedding or a funeral with her knows how she
felt about formal occasions. So Harry and Elise
and I, when we were talking about this, decided
we would just have everyone over and let anyone who wanted to talk about Monica just talk
about her. Maybe share some remembrances
of her. Some of us know each other, some of

us don't. But we're all here because we loved
Monica. (*Pause*) And because we want to pay
tribute to her in a way that might conceivably
not enrage her.

There is some scattered laughter and smiles.

EMILY

I don't want to tell anyone what to think, or how
to feel. And I don't want to kid myself about
the stupid, meaningless way she died. But I
don't want it to become the summation of her
life. Because it's not. When her Lisa died I said
to her, "How can you stand it?" And she said,
"First of all I can't. But I don't want to take away
the twelve years she *did* have, and turn them all
into leukemia. Because they weren't." So I do
think it's important to remember that despite
the fact that she got—ripped *off*. . . that she
was the most fully developed person I personally have ever known. She was also impossible
to get along with, but that's another story.

Everybody laughs.

EMILY

So. Now I've said my little piece. And now I
want to talk a little bit about the first time we
met. She was twenty-one.

Emily stops so as not to cry. There is a long, charged silence.

WOMAN MOURNER

It's OK, Emily.

EMILY

I know . . . ! (*She waits*) And I was *nine-teen* . . . Even though it's impossible for my children to believe I was ever that young.

Emily's nearby college-age kids, a boy and a girl, smile at her. Lisa watches everything from the back.

INT. EMILY'S APARTMENT. LATER. DAY.

Everyone is milling around. Lisa is talking to Emily.

LISA

Emily, thank you so much for letting me be here.

EMILY

Don't be silly, honey. You were sweet to come by—

WOMAN MOURNER

Excuse me. Good bye, Emily. Thank you so much for doing this.

Emily and the Woman Mourner hug each other goodbye.

EMILY

Listen. I still can't believe this is happening . . . !

WOMAN MOURNER

Me neither . . . !

Emily notices Lisa looking at her, waiting. She pulls away.

EMILY

OK, sweetheart . . . (*Pause*) Please don't stand there staring at me, OK?

LISA
(*Startled, embarrassed*)

I'm sorry! I just wanted to say goodbye.

EMILY

It's OK. Thank you for coming. You're very sweet.

LISA

Goodbye.

WOMAN MOURNER

Goodbye.

As Lisa searches for and gets her coat off the coat rack, she hears:

WOMAN MOURNER

Who is that?

EMILY

That's a girl who was passing by at the time of the accident. She was right there when she died, and she wanted to come to the funeral. I told her there was no funeral, but she wanted to come anyway. I wouldn't have done that at her age, would you?

WOMAN MOURNER

No . . .

INT./EXT. CAB (MOVING) NIGHT.

Lisa takes a cab through the lit-up city.

EXT. LISA'S BLOCK. NIGHT.

We hear Lisa on the phone, V.O.

> LISA
> (*V.O.*)
>
> Hi, I'm trying to get a number for one of your
> drivers? . . . His name is Gerald Maretti? He
> drives the 104, I believe . . . Um, it's kind of a
> personal matter. Sorry . . . It's not possible for
> you to confirm a phone number . . . ?

EXT. LISA'S ROOM. NIGHT.

Through her window we see Lisa on the phone. A month-old New
York Times *article about the accident is on her bed. O.C. we hear
Curtis practicing his scales.*

> LISA
>
> No—M A R E T T I . . . What about Brook-
> lyn? . . . You do? . . . Thank you.

*She writes in a note pad, hangs up, and looks at the number. She dials
the phone. It rings once. She hangs up.*

INT. LISA'S ROOM. NIGHT/INT. KARL'S HOUSE. DUSK.

Lisa is on the phone with Karl. WE CUT BETWEEN THEM.

> LISA
>
> Hi Dad.

KARL

Yeah! Hi! How's everything been going?

LISA

OK. How are you?

KARL

Not too bad. Pretty good. I'm sitting here listening to some music. Having a glass of delicious beer.

LISA

That sounds pleasant.

KARL

Yeah. Yeah. How are you? How's the boyfriend situation?

LISA

Well . . . there's this one guy I sort of had something going with. But he kind of has a girlfriend, so . . .

KARL

Uh huh?

LISA

I realize I'm incredibly enthralling . . .

KARL

You are. You're a beautiful girl. *And* you've got brains. That makes you a little dangerous.

LISA

Don't forget mature.

KARL

Well—I'm hoping you're not *too* mature.

LISA

No . . . Don't worry.

KARL

OK, good. That was a good answer.

LISA

Anyway, I do think it's a pretty long-standing relationship . . .

KARL

OK, then you know what? You do nothing. You do absolutely nothing. And one of two things will happen. Either he's gonna start doing *back* flips to get your attention, or you're gonna send him a crystal clear signal that if he *doesn't* do back flips he's not gonna *get* your attention. OK?

LISA

Well, I think he already knows I like him.

KARL	LISA
Uh huh? OK . . . That's OK. Because *now*, if now you *stop* acknowledging him, you just suddenly give him *nothing*,	I think I might have—

he's gonna go *berserk*. Unless
he's just not interested. In
which case, you gotta take
your lumps. OK? Which
is tough.

                    LISA

Well, thanks, Dad. I'll be sure to try out the
technique next time I see him.

                    KARL

OK. Well, everything's OK here . . . A little
slow—

                    LISA

Actually, Dad? I actually have something kind
of serious I want to ask you about . . . I'm kind
of soliciting people I respect for their views
on this . . .

                    KARL

OK. What's up?

EXT. KARL'S HOUSE. DUSK.

*Wider, through the glass doors of Karl's bungalow as he listens to the
story.*

INT. LISA'S ROOM. NIGHT./INT. KARL'S HOUSE. DUSK.

                    LISA

. . . so do you think I should go back to the
police, or what?

KARL

OK, well, first of all, I'm very glad you told me.
Second of all, I think you should let me call my
friend who's a lawyer, just to get some idea of
what the ramifications would be.

ANNETTE, Karl's, girlfriend, 40, lets herself into the house.

ANNETTE	LISA
Hey . . . !	Actually, Dad? Please don't call anybody. Seriously. I appreciate your taking charge and everything, but—Hello?

KARL

Hi babe.

ANNETTE

Did you get my message?

KARL

Um—I got *a* message.

ANNETTE	LISA
About the flowers? For my mother?	Hello . . . ?

KARL

I don't know. Yes. Hold on.
(*To Lisa*) I'm sorry, Annette
just walked in.

LISA

That's OK.

Mark Ruffalo (Maretti)

John Gallagher Jr. (Darren) and Anna Paquin (Lisa)

J. Smith-Cameron (Joan) and Anna Paquin

J. Smith-Cameron

Matt Damon (Mr. Aaron) and Anna Paquin

Anna Paquin and Mark Ruffalo

Anna Paquin

Matt Damon and Anna Paquin

ANNETTE

Who are you talking to?

KARL

I'm—It's—could I just—

LISA

Anyway, I guess I would just like to know later that I would have done the right thing by myself, if you see what I mean. Because I don't think I have so far.

KARL

Uh huh?

LISA

Not that I'm trying to make this woman's horrible death into my own personal moral gymnasium . . .

KARL

Right, well, that's that Shaw quote.

LISA

What?

KARL

The Shaw quote? That great Shaw quote . . . ? The . . . um, "The Englishman sees the world as expressly designed to be his own personal moral gymnasium"? I think it's in one of those wonderful prefaces?

LISA

I don't know where I read it.

ANNETTE

Who is that?

KARL

Uh huh? (*To Annette*) It's Lisa.

ANNETTE   LISA

Oh good. Will you please ask   I—Anyway—
her—

KARL

I'm sorry, Lisa. Hold on one second.

LISA

OK.

KARL
(*To Annette*)

Yes.

ANNETTE

Will you please ask her if there's anything we
don't know about that she won't eat? For the
trip? Because I have to tell the ranch, because
they do all the meals ahead of time—

KARL

Yes: I will: We're just in the middle of something.

ANNETTE

Karl, I was supposed to call them last week. You
said you were gonna call her and you didn't.

So then *I* called her, and she never called me back. So what do you want me to do?

KARL

OK, you know what? I want to talk about this not right now.

ANNETTE

—and if there's anything she can't eat and they put it in the hampers, she's not gonna have anything to eat. The last time she came out here we went to three different places and she couldn't eat anything on the menu.

KARL

I'm going to ask her. I will. We're right in the middle of something.

ANNETTE

OK. Tell her I said Hi.

LISA

Hello?

KARL
(*To Lisa*)

Hi.

INT. LISA'S ROOM. NIGHT.

Lisa puts a new cowboy hat in her luggage. She tries to zip the bag but it won't zip. (This is a dream)

INT. LISA'S ROOM. NIGHT. LATER.

Lisa is asleep. The room is dark. She stirs. She realizes Joan is sitting on the edge of her bed, her back to Lisa.

> LISA
>
> Mom? What's wrong? . . . Did you have a bad show? What time is it?

Joan starts coughing. Blood starts coming out with every cough—

Lisa wakes up in her bed. The room is dark and quiet. She calms down and gets up.

INT. BATHROOM.

She comes in, turns on the light and goes to the sink. She turns on the faucet. She looks down—

BLOOD is streaming out of the faucet and filling the basin.

She looks up. Monica Patterson, the dead woman, is standing behind her in the mirror. Lisa jumps—

INT. LISA'S ROOM. NIGHT.

Lisa wakes up for real this time, sharply, breathing hard, drenched in sweat.

She looks down at the ruled notepad on her bed, with GERALD MARETTI's Brooklyn address and phone number where she wrote it down earlier.

EXT. BROADWAY & 86TH STREET. DAY.

In the criss-crossing flow of Upper West Siders, we see Lisa approach and walk down the steps of a subway station entrance billboarded with a large advertisement for Joan's show.

EXT. BAY RIDGE. DAY.

Lisa emerges from the subway station. The Verrazano Narrows Bridge dominates the background.

EXT. MARETTI'S STREET. DAY.

Lisa turns the unfamiliar corner. Little kids play in the street. She checks the address on the piece of paper.

EXT. MARETTI'S HOUSE. DAY.

She rings the doorbell. Inside she hears kids playing. The door opens. It's MRS. MARETTI, 30s, tough, and very pretty.

> MRS. MARETTI
>
> Hi, can I help you?

> LISA
>
> Hi. I'm sorry to bother you. My name is Lisa Cohen. I was involved in the same accident that Mr. Maretti was involved in a few weeks ago . . .

> MRS. MARETTI
>
> Oh my God, were you? Oh my God, what a thing, huh?

> LISA
>
> Yeah . . . I was just wondering if I could talk to him for a minute. Is he home?

> MRS. MARETTI
>
> Ummmmm, yeah, sure. Whyn't you come in?

INT. MARETTI'S HOUSE. CONTINUOUS.

Lisa follows Mrs. Maretti into the small apartment. From the upstairs, O.C. we HEAR two small BOYS running around and shouting. Maretti is watching TV. Mrs. Maretti goes over and speaks to him, low. He sees Lisa and slowly gets up.

> LISA

Hi. I'm really sorry to bother you . . . We never met. My name is Lisa Cohen . . .

> MARETTI

Yeah . . . What can I do for you?

> LISA

Well . . . do you remember me? From the bus accident?

> MARETTI

I don't know . . . What's this about?

> LISA

Well, would it be OK if I talked to you for a minute?

> MARETTI

What do you want to talk about? I don't understand.

> LISA

I'd just like to talk about the accident for a minute. I don't want anything, and I'm not

here to do anything bad. I just wanted to talk
to you about it.

MARETTI

How did you get my address?

LISA

It's in the phone book. I was gonna call first—

MARETTI

Well, it woulda been better if you woulda
called. We're about to sit down . . .

He looks from Lisa to Mrs. Maretti.

MARETTI

I don't get what, uh . . . Yeah all right. Let's
go outside.

LISA

I'm sorry: Could I use your bathroom?

MARETTI

No, let's just go outside.

MRS. MARETTI

Gerry, let her use the bathroom.

MARETTI

No, I don't want her to use the bathroom. I
don't understand what this is.

MRS. MARETTI

It's right over there, honey. (*Calling up the stairs*) Will you kids settle down, please? I'm not kiddin'!

Lisa goes in the bathroom.

MARETTI	MRS. MARETTI
What's the matter with you?	Who is she?

MARETTI	MRS. MARETTI
She's some girl who was at the accident—	Nothin's the matter with me, let her use the fuckin' bathroom.

INT. BATHROOM. DAY.

Lisa latches the door of the little bathroom. She sits on the toilet and tries to pee. After a minute a tiny amount of pee comes out.

EXT. MARETTI'S HOUSE. DAY.

Maretti, Mrs. Maretti, and Lisa come out.

MARETTI
(*To Mrs. Maretti*)

Honey, just do me a favor, wait inside.

MRS. MARETTI

No. I wanna hear what this is.

LISA

Well . . . If it's OK, I'd rather talk to Mr. Maretti in private.

MRS. MARETTI

No it's not OK.

MARETTI

OK. We're just tryin' to . . . OK: What?

Lisa looks at them, wishing Mrs. Maretti would leave.

LISA

OK. I hope this isn't going to insult you too much . . .

MARETTI

Insult me . . . ?

LISA

. . . I was just wondering if you felt bad at all about what happened.

MARETTI

Do I feel bad about the accident?

LISA

Yeah.

MRS. MARETTI

You know, honey? Are you just upset about the accident . . . ?

LISA

Yes! I'm upset about the accident! I'm very upset about the accident and I wanted to talk to you about it for a minute! Why is that so *strange!?*

MRS. MARETTI

Gerry . . . why don't we all go inside and sit down?

LISA
(*On "why"*)

Could I please talk to you alone?

MRS. MARETTI

OK: What is goin' on here?

MARETTI

Nothin's goin' on here. So whyn't you calm down? Look: Go ahead inside. Let me find out what this is. Meantime whyn't you make sure those kids aren't killin' each other, all right?

MRS. MARETTI

All right.

As Mrs. Maretti goes inside:

MARETTI
(*More jovially*)

No, you know what? Let 'em kill each other. Give us all a rest. (*To Lisa*) All right, Lisa. What.

LISA

I just . . . Well, I just want you to know . . .

She is having trouble speaking.

MARETTI

Yes? What? Speak . . . !

LISA

Well . . . you probably already know, obviously, that I told the police on the police report that I thought the whole thing was an accident . . .

MARETTI

Uh huh. Right. Because it was an accident.

LISA

Well—I mean, I know you didn't do it on *purpose.*

MARETTI

On *purpose* . . . ?

LISA

But it wasn't like . . .

MARETTI

What. (*Pause*) Speak. Talk! What!

LISA

Well . . . I mean . . . We were looking at each other . . .

MARETTI

Who was looking at each other . . . ? You and me?

LISA

Well . . . Yeah . . . I mean . . . not like . . . *romantically* or anything . . .

MARETTI

Romantically . . . !

LISA

OK, scratch that. 'Cause that's not even . . . relevant . . .

MARETTI
(*On "even"*)

You're not comin' through very clearly!

LISA

OK. I can see the way this is.

MARETTI

The way what is? What! Speak to me! What?

LISA

I am—!

MARETTI

Don't drag me outta my house on a Saturday afternoon and then make me stand here pullin' teeth to find out what you're talkin' about. I've got my kids inside: You're an attractive young lady, you show up at the house—Please! Get to the point or go home. Because I don't care enough, frankly, to stand around here tryin'

to figure out what you're doin' here! (*Pause*)
What! What! What! What!

LISA

All right! Well . . . the way I remember the accident is that you were wearing this cowboy hat—

MARETTI

Yes, it's my cowboy hat that I wear sometimes
to amuse myself on the bus, yes. I was probably
wearing my cowboy hat, yes. What.

LISA

If you could just let me . . . ! From my point of
view, I was out that day trying to *buy* a cowboy
hat, so I was waving at you, because I was looking for one . . . and you were kind of waving
back . . . And I know the police already decided
it was No Fault, or No Criminality, or whatever
they call it—

MARETTI

No Criminality, that's right.

LISA

—I *guess* partly because of what I told them.
And I know I was distracting you, but—I *did*
see the bus go through the red light. And that's
when it hit that woman.

MARETTI

OK. I'm gettin' a little confused over here.

LISA

Only nobody *said* that to them. And I just wanted to like, acknowledge with you that that's what happened.

MARETTI

OK. First of all, I don't really know what you mean by wavin' at you . . . What were you, tryin' to catch the bus . . . ?

LISA

No . . . Yes. But I wanted to ask about your—

MARETTI

Maybe I was wavin' at you like, wavin' to say, you know, "Step away from the bus," if the bus was in motion, I would've waved you away for your own safety, but that's all that would be.

LISA

You don't remember looking at me and waving at me?

Mrs. Maretti comes out again.

MARETTI

No. Not really. No.

LISA

Well . . . I think we both remember something different.

MRS. MARETTI

Your brother's on the phone.

MARETTI

Tell him I'll call him back.

Mrs. Maretti goes back inside.

LISA

I'm not trying to get you in trouble.

MARETTI

I know you're not, because you couldn't get me in trouble. Uhhhh, there's no criminality found . . . the report is, uh, final. And that's it.

LISA

So you're just gonna leave it?

MARETTI

I'm gonna leave it, because that's all that it was. If something else would have happened, I'd take it to whatever that was. It was tragic, it was a tragedy. But there's only a certain speed those brakes can react. That's a physical limitation of the machine. I don't know what else to tell you. It was a shock. It's shock. But that's it. You can't bring her back. Cannot bring her back.

LISA

I'm not talking about bringing her back. I'm talking about telling the accident investigators what really happened.

MARETTI

But you already talked to them!

LISA

I know that. But I lied.

MARETTI

You lied.

LISA

Yes. And I can understand if you don't want to
get in trouble, but—

MARETTI

Then how come nobody else saw it?

LISA

I can't help what other people saw—

MARETTI

You would think someone else would see it.

LISA

I only know what *I* saw.

MARETTI

Then why didn't you say something right then?

LISA

Because—when they were asking me what
happened—it seemed like you were kind of
looking at me—like we were saying to each other,
"Let's not say anything about what happened."

MARETTI

Oh, now I *really* don't know what you're talkin' about.

LISA

I can't *prove* that you were doing that—!

Mrs. Maretti comes back outside.

MARETTI

What did I *say* anything to you? Did I *threaten* you?

LISA

No! And I am not blaming you for any of this! All I'm saying is that I didn't really tell the cops what happened—

LISA	MARETTI
—and I didn't want to go back without—	But you told 'em what you saw! You told 'em what you saw! And so did I! Only I'm the one behind the wheel!

MRS. MARETTI

Gerry! Take it easy!

MARETTI
(*To Mrs. Maretti*)

No, you know what? Leave it alone. (*To Lisa*) You wanna ruin my life? Start tellin' 'em about looks, and you waved at me and I had on my cowboy hat, go ahead! You're gonna go back to school and do your *homework* and I'm gonna

lose my *job!* And who's gonna feed my kids?
You? Are you gonna do it? And for *what?!* She's
dead! She's dead! And there's nothin' I can do
to bring her back!

LISA

I just want to say what really happened.

MARETTI

Hey, do whatever you fuckin' want.

MRS. MARETTI

Gerry—!

MARETTI

But those cops are gonna laugh in your fuckin'
face, because *this was not my fault!*

LISA

It was both our fault.

MARETTI

What'd you say?

LISA

It was both our fault.

Maretti digs in his pocket for his cell phone.

MARETTI

Yeah. Don't say that to me again without a lawyer. Gimme your phone number.

MARETTI

What's your number?
Gimme your number. Oh,
you wanna come to my house
like some anonymous person,
I can't get in touch with you?
What's your fuckin' *number,*
Lisa *Cohen!*

LISA

Why? No! Why do you want it?

MRS. MARETTI

Gerry! Take it easy!

LISA

Fine! It's—um—212-555—

MARETTI

Hold on. (*Enters it on his cell phone*) 555—

LISA

—0157. Why do you need it?

MARETTI

Do whatever you're gonna do. I hope you got
a good lawyer.

LISA

Why are you being like this?!

Maretti turns and goes in the house.

MRS. MARETTI

You know this was very traumatic for him!

LISA
(*Furious*)

Yeah, it's almost as bad as getting your *leg* cut off!

INT. SUBWAY (MOVING) DAY.

PUSH IN ON Lisa as she rides back toward Manhattan in the rat-tling subway car.

INT. EMILY'S KITCHEN. DAY.

Emily sits with Lisa at the kitchen table. Emily is staring at her.

EMILY

I don't understand . . .

Pause.

LISA

I guess I was afraid. I didn't know what to do.

EMILY

You didn't know what to do?

LISA

I know it doesn't sound very impressive.

EMILY

Impressive? (*Pause*) All right: I know you're try-ing to do the right thing now. What does your mother say?

LISA

My mother hasn't really been that helpful.

EMILY

What do you mean?

LISA

I mean she's got a lot going on right now and she just hasn't been that interested, I guess.

EMILY

What could she possibly have going on?

LISA

Her show is opening.

EMILY

What do you mean, her show? What show?

LISA

She's in a play.

EMILY

My friend is dead because some guy was looking at your ass and you lied to the police about it, and your mother can't be bothered because she's in a play?

LISA

Well, it's kind of a big deal for her. She has a really big part.

EMILY

OK—I'm gonna talk to a friend of mine who's a lawyer, and you're gonna go talk to the police. Do you want me to go with you?

LISA

No thanks.

EMILY

Do you think maybe you should ask your *mother* to go with you?

LISA

I think I can handle this part myself.

INT. THEATER—BACKSTAGE/ONSTAGE. NIGHT.

Joan waits in the wings. Her CUE LIGHT is lit. It goes OFF. We TRACK onto the stage as she enters.

JOAN

Hey! Let me tell you something, Eliot—

She is interrupted by entrance applause. She waits for it to nearly die down.

JOAN

You want to fire me, go ahead and fire me. Only don't tiptoe around me like some kind of deranged ballerina every time I see you in the fucking hall! Now: Do you have anything to say to me, Eliot?

VICTOR

Um—you're not fired . . . ?

This gets a big laugh from the audience.

JOAN

Oh. (*Abashed, friendly*) What are you guys talking about?

Another big laugh.

IN THE AUDIENCE—Lisa, Curtis, and Ramon sit together, dressed up for opening night. Lisa finds herself smiling, and deliberately stops.

INT. COHEN APARTMENT—LIVING ROOM. MORNING.

Lisa is on the computer. Joan is standing behind her.

> JOAN
>
> Did you find it?

> LISA
>
> Just a minute . . .

> JOAN
>
> Can we just forget it? If they were any good somebody would have called me last night.

> LISA
>
> What do you care what they say about you anyway?

> JOAN
>
> I don't! It's just a lousy feeling. Can't you understand that? If they wrote mean things about you in the newspaper you wouldn't like it. Even if you didn't agree with it, or base your self-esteem on it. Why can't you understand that?

> LISA
>
> I do understand it, because we have this conversation *every time*! You're great in the play,

you're a great actress, everybody thinks you're
great, everything you do is great, you're really
really pretty—

JOAN

Oh shut up.

Lisa finds the New York Times *review online.*

LISA

OK.

JOAN

Did you find it?

LISA

Yes.

Lisa reads.

JOAN

Is it bad?

LISA

Let me read it. (*She reads*) OK, it's really good.

JOAN

Fuck him.

LISA

Oh my God. Listen to this:

JOAN
(*Crossing to Lisa*)

Don't read it to me.

LISA

"*. . . but it is the frankly extraordinary Joan Kaplan who transforms the savage wit of David Holmes' acid comedy-drama into something approaching sheer luminosity . . .*"

JOAN

Get out!

LISA

"*But don't be misled by her feather-light touch and expert comic timing. With the canny* (Has trouble enunciating:) *brav . . .*

JOAN

Bravura?

LISA

Yes.

INT. COHEN APARTMENT—KITCHEN. DAY.

Lisa is eating breakfast and listening to the radio. She hears Joan talking on the phone in the other room, O.C.

RADIO NEWSCASTER	JOAN (O.C.)
—when the seventeen-year-old Palestinian was stopped by Israeli police from board-	No, Lisa read it . . . No, I never read them unless I know there's nothing mean

ing a school bus yesterday
carrying forty pounds of
explosive under her
her jacket—

in them . . . Victor, I wish
you wouldn't speak to me
that way: You *know* I'm Top
of Craft.

Lisa turns up the volume on the radio.

INT. ENGLISH CLASS. DAY.

John is reading from a paperback poetry anthology. On the black-board it says 19TH CENTURY POETS with a list that includes GERARD MANLEY HOPKINS—1844–1889. SLOW PUSH IN on Lisa.

JOHN

"Spring and Fall to a Young Girl," by Gerard
Manley Hopkins. (*Pause*)
"Margaret are you grieving
Over Goldengrove unleaving?
Leaves, like the things of man, you
With your fresh thoughts care for, can you?
Ah! As the heart grows older
It will come to such thoughts colder
By and by, nor spare a sigh
Though worlds of wanwood leafmeal lie,
And yet you *will* weep, and know why.
Now no matter, child, the name:
Sorrow springs are the same.
Nor mouth had, no nor mind, expressed
What heart heard of, ghost guessed:
It is the blight man was born for,
It is Margaret you mourn for."

Silence.

JOHN

Any thoughts? Lisa?

Lisa looks up.

MONTAGE: Lisa takes a cab from the Upper West Side up to the Bronx, passing a variety of New York City neighborhoods.

EXT. HIGHWAY ONE POLICE STATION—THE BRONX. DAY.

Lisa gets out a taxi in front of the large police station nestled in a thicket of trees. There are birds singing and cars whooshing by on the nearby expressway.

INT. HIGHWAY ONE POLICE STATION. DAY.

Lisa walks up to the desk of a 2ND AIS DETECTIVE.

2ND AIS DETECTIVE

Could I help you?

LISA

Um, yeah. Is Detective Mitchell here?

2ND AIS DETECTIVE

No he's not.

LISA

Oh. Um—I talked to him on Monday and he said he'd be here after three. . . .

2ND AIS DETECTIVE

Yeah, he's not back yet. Could I help you with something?

LISA

Um, well, do you know when do you expect him?

2ND AIS DETECTIVE

What's this about?

LISA

I was involved in an accident a few weeks ago—

2ND AIS DETECTIVE

Uh huh?

LISA

And I filled out a report with Detective Mitchell, but wanted to amend the report, so I thought I should—

2ND AIS DETECTIVE

What do you mean amend the report? How do you want to amend it?

LISA

Well, there was something I didn't tell him, and I wanted to tell him, because—

2ND AIS DETECTIVE

So wait, I don't understand. You wanna change your statement?

LISA

Yes! Yes! I want to change my statement. (*Pause*) Yes.

2ND AIS DETECTIVE

Well, you'd usually have to talk to the investigating detective on the case.

LISA

Yes. I know. That's why I asked to see Detective
Mitchell. Who said he'd be here now. Which
he's not. So . . .

2ND AIS DETECTIVE
(*On "so"*)

You remember the case number?

LISA

No. Sorry. It was that woman Monica Patterson,
who got run over by the bus, on Broadway—it
was in a lot of the newspapers . . .

2ND AIS DETECTIVE

OK, yeah, sure, OK. Sit down, sit down.

LISA
(*Sitting*)

Thank you. I—

2ND AIS DETECTIVE

You know the case is closed.

LISA

I assume it was. But part of the reason it's
closed is because of my statement. And the
statement I gave—

2ND AIS DETECTIVE

Because of your statement?

Another male detective walks by, behind Lisa. The two men exchange a glance referring to Lisa being a cute girl.

LISA

Yes.

2ND AIS DETECTIVE

What do you mean it was closed because of your statement?

LISA

I mean—

2ND AIS DETECTIVE

The DA's office closes the case. You don't close the case. The DA's office closes the case.

LISA

I'm sure it does. I obviously didn't mean I personally closed the case, like, *legally*. I meant that what I said was probably instrumental in getting the case closed, because I was the—

2ND AIS DETECTIVE

What's your name, honey?

LISA

Lisa Cohen.

2ND AIS DETECTIVE

OK—

LISA

Don't call me honey, OK?

Pause.

2ND AIS DETECTIVE

OK.

LISA

Are you not gonna help me now that I said that?

2ND AIS DETECTIVE

Look—*What's* your name?

LISA

Lisa Cohen!

2ND AIS DETECTIVE

OK Lisa, first thing, you're gonna calm down—

LISA

I'm calm right now!

2ND AIS DETECTIVE

OK. Just checking. Second thing—Oh! Here he is: Your knight in shining armor.

Mitchell has just come in. Lisa gets up.

MITCHELL

This guy been givin' you a hard time?

LISA

No.

INT. HIGHWAY ONE POLICE STATION—MITCHELL'S DESK. LATER

Lisa sits across from Mitchell.

MITCHELL

So now you're sayin' he ran the light.

LISA

Yes. He wasn't even looking at the *road*. And I was definitely trying to get his *attention* . . .

MITCHELL

No no no, yeah: I get the picture. So you're flirtin' with this guy, he's wavin' at you, he runs the light, hits the decedent, the both of youse lie to me on both of your statements, and then somewheres in there you turn around, decide the guy belongs in jail. That right? (*Pause*) That about right?

LISA

I don't have any control over if he goes to jail or not. I certainly have my hopes. I just want to set the record straight, so that if he gets away with this I won't have been a part of it.

MITCHELL

And what do you think I should do with *you?*

Pause.

LISA

Do whatever you want. I know what I did.

MITCHELL

OK. Well. Before we do anything, Lisa, anybody will tell you that just because he ran a red light is not a criminal offense.

LISA

Even if he kills someone?

MITCHELL
(*On "kills"*)

Even if you cause an accidental death—that's right. For this to be a criminal offense, the law says you need two aggravating circumstances. Like he ran a red light *and* he was speeding. Or he ran a red light *and* he was—

LISA
(*On the 2nd "red"*)

So he's not liable to be prosecuted for manslaughter? Or second degree murder?

MITCHELL

No. He could be charged with reckless driving, and fillin' out a false police report. Which, that's no joke—

LISA

That's *unbelievable!* What does he have to do?
Kill her on purpose?

MITCHELL

Yes. Because that's the definition of murder.
Killin' somebody on purpose. You're not sayin'
he ran her over on purpose, are you? (*Pause*)
Are you?

Pause.

LISA

No.

*Pause. Lisa wipes her eyes and looks away. She tries not to cry. Mitchell
watches her. He shifts in his chair uncomfortably. Finally:*

MITCHELL

All right—look . . . Why don't I take another
statement . . . and, uh . . . We'll look into it,
OK?

LISA

You're kidding.

MITCHELL

No. I'll go over it with my sergeant, probably
pull this guy in again. Re-interview him. Put a
little pressure on him. See what he says.

LISA

Thank you . . . ! *Thank* you . . .

EXT. CENTRAL PARK. DAY.

Lisa and Becky are smoking pot on a rock in a shallow grassy slope, giggling.

LISA
(*Holding in smoke*)

. . . Yeah, because the Central Park Conservatory or whatever it's called put up about five hundred miles worth of these cheap shitty-looking fences all over the park. Which is totally antithetical to what the park was originally designed for.

She exhales and hands Becky the joint.

BECKY

We are totally gonna miss the game. Oh my God, it's John . . . ! It's John!

They try to hide the joint from John, the English teacher, who is approaching them. He stops. Pause.

LISA

Hi John.

BECKY

Hi John. (*Pause*) Want some?

They giggle.

JOHN

Come on, guys . . . ! You can't be smokin' a j. on your way to a school soccer game! Now come on!

LISA

Sorry.

BECKY

We're really sorry.

John stares at them, then turns and walks away.

LISA
(*Stage whisper*)

OK: How about how he's like, "Smokin' a j.?"

BECKY	LISA
Yeah . . . ! Let's go over to John's house and smoke a "j."	Like, "You can't be smokin' a j."

They burst out LAUGHING.

CU: The back of John's embarrassed reddening grown-up neck as he keeps walking away.

EXT. CENTRAL PARK WEST. DAY.

Lisa walks along the Park side of the street, somewhat stoned, enjoying the sunshine. She sees Mr. Aaron approaching on a bike. She spits out her chewing gum and smiles as he bikes up to her and stops.

LISA

Hi, Mr. Aaron . . . !

MR. AARON

How are you, Lisa?

LISA

I'm pretty damn good. How are you?

MR. AARON

I'm all right, I'm all right . . . Tell me something. Whatever happened with that situation?

LISA

Oh . . . I'm working on it. I'll tell you all about it sometime . . . (*Squinting at him in the sunshine*) Hey, what kind of a bike is that?

MR. AARON

Um, a Trek.

LISA

I'm supposed to take a horseback riding trip with my father over Christmas break and I was just wondering, does it bear any resemblance to riding a bicycle?

MR. AARON

Um, as far as I know, no, it doesn't, no . . .

LISA

But you must have ridden a lot of horses.

MR. AARON

What makes you say so?

LISA

Aren't you from Texas, or Wyoming, or someplace like that?

MR. AARON

Someplace like what?

LISA

You know: Not New York.

MR. AARON

I'm actually from Terre Haute, Indiana. But don't let me overwhelm you with superfluous details.

LISA

God, so what are you doing at a New York private school teaching geometry to a bunch of overprivileged liberal Jews?

MR. AARON

Well . . . I wanted to be a teacher . . . So that's what I did . . . I came here and I'm a teacher. (*Pause*) Anyway—

He starts to go.

LISA

Before you go, I am actually thinking of getting one of these. Can I try it? Just for one second?

MR. AARON

All right.

LISA

Thanks.

Mr. Aaron gets off the bike.

MR. AARON

You want me to adjust the seat?

LISA

Thank you.

She watches him while he adjusts the seat for her. She bikes away awkwardly, turns around, and bikes back toward him, wobbling badly.

LISA

I like your bicycle . . . ! Can I have it?

MR. AARON

No!

She tries to stop right in front of him but skids, and he catches her hard by the arms to stop her.

MR. AARON

OK. Off.

LISA

Can I just ask you how is it possible that I am totally in love with you and you have almost no interest in me whatsoever?

MR. AARON

Can I have my bike back please?

As she dismounts and he takes the bike and gets on it:

LISA

I can tell you like me . . . It's not like I'm a *virgin*, if that's what you're worried about . . .

LISA

I'm not even close.

MR. AARON

I can't even be having this conversation with you . . . !

LISA

It's not my fault if I revere you as a god!

He laughs or smiles in spite of himself, and starts to bike away.

LISA

Oh my God. I made you laugh! I am so happy right now.

MR. AARON

I'll see you in class!

We pull away with him as she watches him go.

INT. COHEN APARTMENT—LIVING ROOM. DUSK.

Lisa is flipping through a magazine. Joan is getting ready to leave.

JOAN

. . . someone named Emily called, and Detective Mitchell called from the Accident Investigation Squad. Is that the one you talked to? (*Pause*) What's going on? Did you ever go back and see him?

LISA

I'd rather not talk about it when you have one
foot out the door. I'll tell you later, if that's OK.

JOAN

Of course it is. (*Pause*) Who's Emily?

LISA

She's the friend of the woman who died, the
one who had the funeral . . .

JOAN

Oh yeah, OK. Well, her number's by the phone.

LISA

OK, thanks.

*Joan waits, looking down at her. Lisa turns the page of her magazine
and keeps reading.*

JOAN

All right . . . I'm gonna go.

LISA
(*Looks up*)

Have a good show.

JOAN

Thank you. (*Calling*) Goodbye, Curtis!

No answer. Joan heads for the door.

INT. BUILDING HALLWAY. NIGHT.

Joan comes down the hall and pushes the elevator button. She sees her reflection in the little round elevator window. She looks old to herself. She touches under her chin.

INT. ELEVATOR. CONTINUOUS.

Joan gets in. The door shuts. She leans her head against the wall and bursts into tears. The elevator stops with a DING. She wipes her eyes quickly. A woman NEIGHBOR comes in.

> NEIGHBOR

Hello . . . !

> JOAN
> (*Smiles*)

Hello.

> NEIGHBOR

Congratulations on the show . . . !

> JOAN

Thank you.

> NEIGHBOR

That was such a wonderful review . . . ! And I read somewhere it might be going to Broadway?

> JOAN

Supposedly. In March.

> NEIGHBOR

God! Exciting . . . !

JOAN

Yeah, it's going well. Knock wood.

INT. COLUMBUS AVENUE RESTAURANT. DAY.

Lisa, Emily, and DAVE, a good natured, successful lawyer in his 30s, are at an outside table. A loud procession of cars, trucks, vans, buses, bicycles, motorcycles, and pedestrians pass by down Columbus Avenue in the sunshine.

EMILY

Lisa, Dave is one of my best friends. He's a terrific lawyer and if he doesn't know what to do himself he'll certainly know someone we can talk to.

LISA

OK, great.

A FEW MINUTES LATER—

They are drinking iced tea or sparkling water. Lisa smokes.

DAVE

When someone is killed it's what you call a Wrongful Death Suit, which is a statutory case, which just means there's a statute passed by the legislature which gives you the right to bring the case.

LISA

As opposed to what?

DAVE

As opposed to Common Law, which is law made by judges. Which is why the damages are limited.

LISA

I don't understand.

EMILY

Look, just skip that part. We don't care about that.

LISA

I thought we were trying to get the police to arrest this guy . . . !

DAVE

No—the police are not, uh—

LISA	EMILY
Why not? They told me they were gonna look into it again.	Dave doesn't think the police are gonna—

DAVE

I'm just telling you that even if they do, there is no way in this world they are gonna recommend to the DA that they charge this guy. That's why—

LISA
(*On "That's"*)

So what can we do?

DAVE

Well. I'm—

LISA

Sorry.

DAVE	EMILY
That's OK—	That's OK, honey . . .

DAVE

I'm just getting to that. You can't do anything unless you're a relative—

EMILY

She didn't have any relatives—

EMILY	DAVE
—except for those idiots in Arizon . . .	—or—hang on a minute— unless you're the executor of her estate—

EMILY

I *am* the executor of her estate.

DAVE

—which is Emily. I know.

EMILY

So good.

DAVE

Yes. This is good. Because the executor of the estate *can* bring a Wrongful Death Suit, but

the beneficiary has to be a relative. So let me
explain about *that:*

Lisa and Emily re-settle themselves in their chairs.

DAVE

In a Wrongful Death Suit you can sue for Pain
and Suffering, Pecuniary Losses, Loss of Support or Services . . . And also what's called
Care, Comfort and Society: Like advice, coun-
seling of the parent that the kids aren't gonna
get anymore . . .

LISA

You can really sue for that?

DAVE

Yeah, and that's probably what we would do:

LISA

So—I don't understand. Who are we suing?
The bus driver?

DAVE

Well, no, because the bus driver wouldn't have
any money. You basically sue everybody and
hope something sticks. The person who pays
would be the MTA's insurance company.

LISA

But do you think the driver would get fired?

DAVE

No. Not necessarily.

LISA

Even if all the facts came out at the trial?

DAVE

Maybe. I don't know.

EMILY

But how much could they be liable for?

DAVE

It depends: If she was alive—

EMILY

How badly do you think we could ever hurt them?

DAVE

—if she was alive, and in a lot of pain, for an extended period of time, they give more money for that.

They both look at Lisa.

LISA

I'd say she was alive for ten minutes.

DAVE

And I gather in a lot of pain?

LISA

Her leg was cut off.

DAVE

Yes—obviously. And—but was she conscious? Awake, the whole time?

LISA

I'm sorry, Emily. (*To Dave*) Yeah, awake.

EMILY

That's OK.

DAVE

Well, if she was in a lot of pain for that long . . . I don't know . . . maybe three hundred thousand or a half a million dollars to get a sustainable verdict? A brain damaged baby would be three million. But the truth is, Lisa, after all's said and done, it's not a very good case.

LISA

Why not?

DAVE

Because it's your word against his, and because you already lied on your first deposition. A red light case is a fifty-fifty proposition already. And with only one eyewitness, with two conflicting statements? *I* wouldn't take that case.

Lisa and Emily look at each other. Emily turns to Dave.

EMILY

Nobody really cares about getting a lot of money here . . .

DAVE

I understand that—

EMILY

. . . We just want this prick to *suffer.* And we
want the bus company to take responsibility
for *hiring* this guy.

DAVE
(*Starts to speak*)

LISA

Anyway, can't I explain why I lied the first time?
It's not like I'm trying to get any money for
myself.

DAVE

That's true . . . Since she has no financial interest she can't be impeached for bias.

EMILY

Impeached for *what?*

DAVE

She can't have her credibility attacked on financial grounds, because the jury knows you're
not getting any money if you win.

LISA

So that's something, isn't it?

EMILY

But do you really think we know what that means?

DAVE

I'm sorry. That's what it's called.

EMILY

But who are you *talking* to? You *know* we don't know what that means. It's like you're not really concentrating.

DAVE

I just—

EMILY

You're not concentrating!

DAVE

I—don't know. I am concentrating. I'm just thinking out loud.

Dave sits back, angry.

EMILY

OK. All right. I'm sorry . . . I'm sorry! (*To Lisa*) He wasn't always a lawyer, you know. He used to be a very nice little boy.

Dave laughs.

DAVE

All right . . . Anyway . . .

LISA

Anyway, the whole point is to get—

EMILY

Is to fucking *get* this guy!

LISA

No, it's to get him out from behind the wheel of a *bus*!

DAVE

Did she know she was dying? (*Pause*) I only ask because the terror of knowing you're dying raises the damages.

Pause.

LISA

I think she had a pretty good idea.

DAVE

If she had lived for a couple of days it would make the case better . . . I know this sounds horrible, but this is what it comes down to . . .

EMILY

I know. We know, Dave. That's OK.

Silence. The waitress brings their food. Dave starts to eat. Emily watches him for a moment.

EMILY

I would just like *somebody* to take responsibility for what *happened*.

DAVE

I understand that, Emily. But no matter how you slice it, the fact that Lisa lied on her first statement is a disaster for your lawyer . . .

Lisa looks down. Dave looks around for a waiter.

INT. ENGLISH CLASS. DAY.

John is walking back and forth, reading aloud from King Lear. *Lisa is very disengaged from the discussion.*

JOHN
(*Reading*)

"As flies to wanton boys are we to the gods. They kill us for their sport." (*Pause*) "As flies to wanton boys are we to the gods. They kill us for their *sport*." (*Pause*) What do you *make* of that? (*Pause*) Lisa? (*Pause*) Lisa!

LISA

I don't know.

JOHN

You know what, Lisa? That's not good enough. That's not good enough. Shakespeare wrote something: What's your response? And don't tell me you don't have one because I don't buy it.

LISA

I don't really have a lot to say. It seems pretty self-evident to me.

He looks at her for a moment, then turns toward the other students.

JOHN

Matthew?

MATTHEW

I think it *is* self-evident. I think he's saying that
human beings don't mean any more to the
gods than flies do to little boys who like to
torture them for fun. Like as far as the gods are
concerned we're just ants. Nothing. (*Turning
to Darren like a newscaster:*) Darren?

The class laughs.

DARREN
(*Responding in kind*)

Thank you, Matthew. Yeah, I agree. Only it's
not Shakespeare saying it: It's Gloucester.
Maybe another character would have a different point of view.

JOHN

OK: That's a valid point. Just because Shakespeare has one of his characters say it doesn't
mean he personally agrees with it. Yes: David?

DAVID

Yeah, maybe Shakespeare isn't saying the gods
don't care about us. Maybe he's saying there's
a higher consciousness that we can't see. That
the gods' perception of reality is so much more
developed than ours, that compared to *their*

perception, *our* perceptions are like comparing flies to boys.

JOHN

OK . . . I don't think that's what he's getting
at . . . I think what he's getting at here is a very
dark view of the arbitrary nature of human
suffering.

DAVID

But maybe he's not. Maybe he's comparing
human consciousness to divine consciousness,
and he's saying that even though it seems to
us that human suffering is just arbitrary, that's
just because we're limited by our viewpoint.

JOHN

OK, but—I still don't think that's what he's
trying to say. Um . . .

DAVID

No, like if you say they kill us for their sport,
when our perception of the gods is so meager
that we can't even tell what they're doing, then
how can we be so arrogant as to think that they
would bother to kill us for their sport?

JOHN
(*Lost*)

I don't know . . . Um—Monica?

MONICA

I don't think that's what he's saying at all. I think he's saying the gods don't give a shit about human beings and they just kill and torture us for fun.

Several hands go up. John starts to call on Anthony.

JOHN

OK—

DAVID
(*Interrupting, oblivious*)

But if the gods' consciousness is so much more developed than ours that we seem like flies to them, then how can we be sure what they have in mind for us or why they do anything?

JOHN

David, I think you've made your point. But it's not what Shakespeare meant. Scholarly opinion is pretty consistent—

DAVID

Scholarly opinion . . . !

JOHN

—that he's trying to say something about human suffering here—

DAVID

But what are you saying? A thousand Frenchmen can't be wrong?

JOHN

No, I'm *not* saying that. But I would like to move on—

DAVID

But I think he *is* saying that, because he's comparing human consciousness to flies, and he's saying that we can't see the truth around us because our consciousness is undeveloped.

JOHN

No David, you're wrong! That's not what Shakespeare meant! He says it somewhere else in the play, but I don't want to get hung up on this any more because it's not what Shakespeare meant! And I would really like to move on.

David laughs derisively.

INT. COHEN APARTMENT—KITCHEN. DAY.

Lisa is on the phone.

LISA

Yes, Detective Mitchell please? . . . My name is Lisa Cohen? . . . C O H—Yes, I'll hold.

INT. SQUAD ROOM. DAY.

Mitchell picks up the phone. WE CUT BETWEEN THEM.

MITCHELL

Detective Mitchell.

LISA

Oh, hi, it's Lisa Cohen calling.

MITCHELL

Hi Lisa, what can I do for you?

LISA

Well, I was just wondering what ever happened, if anything, with the case. You said you might re-interview the bus driver . . .

MITCHELL

Yes, we did: We brought him back in—

LISA

You did? What happened?

MITCHELL

Well, he basically stuck to his original represen-tation, and that was pretty much it. I brought it up with my sergeant, but he agrees with me we still don't have enough to charge this guy, so there's really not a lot more we can do at this point.

LISA

But how did you ask the questions?

MITCHELL

Excuse me?

LISA

He's obviously not gonna change his statement if you just *ask* him, like really *politely*:
Why would he? We already know he's a liar.

MITCHELL

Hey, you know, Lisa, in the old days we'd just
throw him in the back with a rubber hose and
we'd get whatever answer we want out of him.
But fortunately we don't do that kind of thing
anymore—

LISA

Yeah, not to white people.

MITCHELL

Excuse me?

LISA

You don't do it to white people. Anyway, I'm
not saying you—

MITCHELL

We don't do it to *who*?

LISA

Oh my *God*.

MITCHELL

First of all, I don't know why you're bringin'
the guy's race into it. There's forty thousand
cops in this city—

LISA

Yes, thank you, yes.

MITCHELL

—and I hate to disillusion you, but most of 'em are pretty good guys, just tryin' to do their job. Bottom line is the DA's not gonna take this case. Now, you could talk to my sergeant if you want to, but—

LISA

Yes, I would.

MITCHELL

Well, I will patch you through then.

INT. COHEN HALLWAY/KITCHEN. DUSK.

Joan, dressed to go out, comes out of her bedroom and down the hall and she lingers in the kitchen doorway listening to Lisa, who is on the phone.

LISA

So there's no way to appeal—

SERGEANT
(*Over the phone, flat*)

There's nothin' to appeal. There's no case.

LISA

But how do you know Detective Mitchell interrogated him aggressively enough if you weren't *there?*

> JOAN

What's going on?

Lisa waves her away.

EXT. RAMON'S TERRACE. DUSK.

Joan and Ramon are having drinks and looking at his view of the Upper West Side across Central Park.

> JOAN

—so funny: it's the same show, but now they all read how great it is, we get these big standing ovations every night, and it's the exact same show as before.

> RAMON

But why do you put yourself down? It's a wonderful show and a wonderful performance.

> JOAN

No, it's not—I'm not putting myself down. It's just that the audience always reacts differently if they've been told it's good. A lot of actors have that experience.

> RAMON

Mm hm?

She takes a few steps away.

> JOAN

I love this view . . . (Pause) You know, Ramon . . . this may sound very stupid to you, but do

you ever worry that we don't have very much
in common?

RAMON

What do you mean?

JOAN

Well, I don't mean to sound dissatisfied, or
disgruntled. But I feel like we're always misun-
derstanding each other. Do you feel that way
at all? Or am I just completely off the beam?

RAMON

I don't think we should talk about that, Joan.

JOAN

You don't? Well . . . I think it's kind of important or I wouldn't have brought it up.

RAMON

Joan . . . I like you very much. But let's not talk
about what you are like, and what I am like.
That never makes a good result. Talk about it
with your friends.

JOAN

My friends . . . ?

RAMON

Yes.

He sips his drink. Joan doesn't know what to say. Silence.

RAMON

May I show you some pictures of my boys?

JOAN
(*Nonplussed*)

Sure.

INT. RAMON'S LIVING ROOM. NIGHT.

Ramon and Joan are in the beautiful living room, on the sofa, looking at pictures.

RAMON

That's a little place we used to go on holiday, two hours outside of Cartagena . . . My family is all there still, but Rodrigo is studying in London, and Hector is in Geneva. I'm sure they will go back eventually, because they would like to do something for their country. But it's a worry, because it's very bad there now.

JOAN

Yeah . . . I haven't really been following it.

RAMON

It's a big mess. Last year I helped to found an organization to work with children whose families have been killed, or the parents have been kidnapped. We try to find them homes, preferably in Colombia, because if we lose our young people, that's it: That's the future. We have raised a lot of money, but it's hard to see the solution.

JOAN

Yeah. God . . . I wish I knew more about it . . . I feel kind of ignorant about your whole world . . .

RAMON

You think it would be better if we knew about all the same things?

JOAN

Not really, not exclusively. It's just unusual. Don't you think it's unusual?

RAMON

Not for me.

JOAN

I guess you travel a lot. I've only been out of the country a few times in my whole life.

RAMON

You should travel more.

JOAN

I know. I've always wanted to travel. But you don't make a lot of money in the theater . . . It's just a little difficult with two kids and no husband. My ex-husband—

RAMON

Karl.

JOAN

Yes. Karl. Very good. You remembered. Karl is very generous with the kids when he can be, but he's struggling too . . . He directs commercials, and now he's trying to produce them . . . Anyway, I'm not ignorant because I enjoy it.

RAMON

I don't say you're ignorant.

Joan sighs. Silence.

RAMON

Do you think Lisa would be interested in acting?

JOAN

No, I don't. I actually think she has a lot of contempt for it. But maybe that's just the age . . .

RAMON

She would prefer the world with no plays? No films . . . ?

JOAN

Oh . . . Who knows?

They look at each other.

RAMON

Would you like to see a picture of my mother?

> JOAN

Sure.

> RAMON

These are all my aunts and uncles . . . See? Big
family . . .

> JOAN

Mmm.

*She moves a little closer to him, and watches his face as he looks at
the picture.*

EXT. MIDTOWN. DAY.

*Lisa waits at a light on 6th Avenue and the 50s. The light changes
and she walks down the midday Midtown street, against and along
with the bustling flow of pedestrians and traffic.*

INT. DAVE'S LAW FIRM—STAIRCASE/OFFICE. DAY.

*Dave walks Lisa and Emily into his office. The view of the city is
spectacular, the law firm very fancy.*

> DAVE

So after I talked to you guys I called this P.I. I
know and I asked him to—

> EMILY

You called a what? A what?

> DAVE

Private Investigator—to see if he could find
anything out about your bus driver—

LISA

Really?

DAVE   EMILY

Yeah: So he—   *Dave!*

DAVE

Wait, let me tell you what he said . . . !

INT. DAVE'S LAW OFFICE. DAY.

Dave sits at his desk across from Emily and Lisa in his beautifully furnished office, which commands a lofty view of midtown.

DAVE

. . . so *he* called this guy he knows who used to be a cop for the MTA . . . Did you know the MTA have their own police? The MTA police? They have their own uniforms—

EMILY

Yeah? Yeah? Yeah?

DAVE   EMILY

And—Just a minute!   Jesus Christ! What do we
                                give a fuck about the MTA
                                police and their uniforms?!

DAVE
(*Unfazed*)

—so this guy got someone to let him sneak a look at your guy's file. And it turns out he's had two previous accidents—less than two years apart—

EMILY

What?

DAVE

—*but,* that he's never been cited or disciplined, just moved around to different shifts—

EMILY

Are you fucking kidding me?

LISA

Why does this not shock me?

DAVE

Because Surprise Surprise, his brother-in-law is a very big muckety-muck in the Transit Workers Union—

EMILY

O-Kay . . .

DAVE

—and if you read the paper, you'll know they're going through a protracted labor dispute at the MTA right now, and according to my PI, the management doesn't want to aggravate the situation by firing this guy.

LISA

This is making me sick.

DAVE

I know, but what it means, Lisa, is that we have
a case.

LISA

We do?

DAVE

What it means, in fact, is that we have a very
good case, because we can sue for what's called
Negligent Retention. Which means they should
have known the guy was a bad risk and was irresponsible and they negligently retained him
until he finally killed somebody.

EMILY

And you can prove that?

DAVE

Sure, because we can subpoena their Personnel records, which we already know contain
damaging information, because my investigator got a look at them beforehand.

EMILY

But you wouldn't be our lawyer, right?

DAVE

No no. Oh no.

LISA

Why not?

DAVE

EMILY

I'm not a personal injury litigator. I don't know enough about it. I would lose.

It's not his area.

EMILY

But you could recommend someone?

DAVE

Sure. (*Pause*) I know a guy who's very good. His name is Russel Deutsch. He's not a sleaze-bag. Very experienced. Let me give you his number . . .

EMILY

Dave, thank you so much.

LISA

Really. My God.

DAVE

But you gotta get that crazy cousin on board because she's gonna be your beneficiary.

EMILY

She's not gonna want to come to New York, I can tell you that right now.

DAVE

If you win she gets anywhere from three to five hundred thousand dollars. She's coming to New York.

LISA

You're *awesome.*

EXT. 6TH AVENUE. DAY.

Lisa and Emily walk up the busy avenue together.

LISA

What's with Monica and her cousin?

EMILY

Oh, Monica's father left some money to Abigail's kids and he made Monica the executor
of the estate, because he didn't want Abigail
and her idiot husband to get their hands on
the money before the kids were grown up.
For which Abigail rewarded her by badgering
her about it on the phone for fifteen years:
Always trying to borrow money against the
estate, nasty phone calls, nasty letters, every
month for fifteen years until Abigail's daughter turned twenty-one and got married. Then
Monica goes to the wedding, in fucking *Arizona,* and Abigail *literally* won't speak to her.
She's a dream.

LISA

So that's who we're getting the money for?

EMILY

It's not who we're getting it for, it's who we're
getting it from.

INT. DEUTSCH'S OFFICE. DAY.

Emily and Lisa sit with RUSSEL DEUTSCH, 50s. His Lower Manhattan 30th floor law office is smaller and less expensive-looking than Dave's.

> DEUTSCH

First thing we do is we file a summons and a complaint against the MTA. They get twenty days to respond, and when they do we can make our Discovery requests: Accident reports, personnel records, et cetera. But you gotta realize it's gonna take some time. The law says you have to get a court date within a year. Usually it takes about six. Depending.

> LISA

Six years?

> DEUTSCH

Depending, yes.

> EMILY

Now, I mentioned to Dave I have a friend who writes for the Metro section of the *Times* . . .

> DEUTSCH

Yes: Now this, if it could really happen, this changes everything in our favor. If they think there's gonna be adverse publicity, especially in the *New York Times*, they're gonna want to settle right away, soon as possible, and as *quietly* as possible—

EMILY

So they'd make it a condition that . . .

DEUTSCH

It's usually done, you get the money but you can't talk about it. Nobody knows the terms.

LISA

So what good does that do?

DEUTSCH

You get the money. (*Pause*) Is that bad? (*Pause*) This is how our society punishes people for doing bad things.

LISA

By getting money from their employers' insurance companies?

DEUTSCH

Yes. It's called Punitive Damages.

Pause.

LISA

Could we insist they fire the driver? As part of the settlement?

DEUTSCH

Yes, sure, why not?

LISA

But is that something people do?

DEUTSCH

Sure. It's one of your conditions.

EMILY

Great.

LISA

And you think we're gonna win? They're gonna
settle?

DEUTSCH

Oh they're gonna settle.

LISA

This is—

Emily and Lisa take hands and squeeze.

INT. COHEN APARTMENT—LIVING ROOM. LATER THAT DAY.

*Joan is reading Lisa's report card and an accompanying letter. Lisa
comes in and stops short.*

JOAN

I want to talk to you.

LISA

I take it that's my report card?

JOAN

It sure is.

INT. EMILY'S APARTMENT—FRONT DOOR. DAY.

Emily opens her front door for Joan and Lisa.

JOAN

Hi. I'm Joan. It's nice to meet you.

EMILY

Nice to meet you too. Come on in.

LISA
(*Sardonically*)

Hi Emily.

INT. EMILY'S APARTMENT—LIVING ROOM. DAY.

Emily, Joan, and Lisa settle on the sofa and chairs.

JOAN

. . . I had a friend who used to live on this block,
at 262 . . . ?

EMILY

Oh . . . ?

JOAN

Yeah, I don't know if you know her. Cheryl
Rowan? She's a physiotherapist?

EMILY

No, I don't know her.

LISA

I think about a thousand people must . . .

JOAN

What?

LISA

Nothing . . .

EMILY

Lisa says you're in a play, Joan?

JOAN

Oh—Yeah . . .

LISA

You should go see it, it's really good.

JOAN

Well, the play is great, and it's a really nice cast . . .

LISA

She's just being modest. She's gonna win every award in New York.

JOAN

Oh—all that stuff's a long way off.

EMILY

I don't go to the theater very much.

JOAN

Well, it's just nice, because you can work a long time in the theater and play really good parts without getting a lot of recognition. And even though you don't necessarily do it for that as your primary motive, it is very nice when people do notice something you've done.

EMILY

Uh huh . . .

JOAN

I was on a television show a few years ago, and I had been doing theater all my life, and suddenly all my relatives started calling me up to congratulate me because they thought I finally "made it." And it was really just this dumb show that paid the bills for a while . . .

LISA

That show was so stupid.

JOAN

It wasn't *that* bad . . . Anyway: I realize this is horribly embarrassing for Lisa, but I really wanted to meet you, Emily, because you've frankly become such a big part of Lisa's life, and I don't want to be intrusive, but this whole court case seems to be suddenly dominating everything and I can't get Lisa to tell me anything about it—

LISA

That's not true.

JOAN

Well, I can't . . . ! And I want you to know, Lisa, that I'm very, very proud of you for pursuing this the way you have. But I can't let you pursue it to the point where it's taking over your life or interfering with your school work. (*To Emily*) It's really come down to a question of homework. Lisa is on a half-scholarship at her school. And I know she feels a real sense of responsibility about what happened—

LISA

Yeah, I do.

JOAN

I know you do. I know you do. But you can't not do your homework, and you can't throw away your scholarship because of it.

LISA

I'm not. My grades slipped a little. They'll get better. Anyone can do their homework. You just sit down and do it. I've been distracted. I'll stop.

JOAN

All right—

LISA

We didn't need to have a big conference about it.

JOAN

It's not a big conference, I just want to know what's going on. And I wanted to meet Emily . . . (*To Emily*) I know it's a little awkward . . . !

EMILY

Don't apologize. If Lisa hasn't been keeping you apprised of what's been going on, I think she should. You should.

LISA

There's nothing to keep her apprised of. We're just waiting for them to schedule the Discovery conference.

JOAN

Now what is that?

LISA

Mom? It really doesn't matter.

EMILY

A Discovery conference is a meeting with the court where they sign an order authorizing our lawyer to begin getting the personnel records, interviewing witnesses, talking to Monica's cousin . . .

JOAN

OK, now where does she fit in?

EMILY

She gets the money.

EXT. MIDTOWN HOTEL. DAY.

ABIGAIL BERWITZ, 40s, gets out of the taxi. The driver opens the trunk and takes out her matching travel bags.

INT. DEUTSCH'S OFFICE. DAY.

Abigail sits with Deutsch.

> DEUTSCH
>
> How would you describe the relationship over-all? Did you talk on the phone a lot? Were there a lot of visits—

> ABIGAIL
>
> I would say we talked on the phone a couple of times a month at least. Sometimes more than that . . . I would call her, she would call me . . .

> DEUTSCH
>
> And what were the nature of these conversations?

> ABIGAIL
>
> Oh, family stuff, mostly. Her family, my kids . . .

> DEUTSCH
>
> And she would advise you about your family? That kind of thing?

> ABIGAIL
>
> Oh, I would say so, yes.

> DEUTSCH
>
> Would you have any phone records? Or—

ABIGAIL

I have all my phone bills, if that's what you mean.
I didn't record the actual conversations . . .

DEUTSCH

No no—

ABIGAIL
(*Produces her phone bills*)

You'll see we talked on the phone quite frequently.

DEUTSCH

OK, that's terrific. I see you came prepared . . . !

ABIGAIL

Well, I wanted to bring everything.

DEUTSCH

Now, when they take your deposition you're
gonna say the same thing you just told me.
Talk about the relationship . . .

ABIGAIL

Uh huh?

DEUTSCH

Kind of advice she used to give you . . .

ABIGAIL

OK . . . ?

INT. MIDTOWN RESTAURANT. DAY.

*Emily, Lisa, and Abigail sit over their lunch. Abigail is drinking a
white wine.*

ABIGAIL

Now, Emily, where did you find this lawyer?

EMILY

He was recommended by a friend.

ABIGAIL

I'm asking because my husband knows a real
good New York lawyer, and I'm not entirely
comfortable with someone that no one has
ever heard of—

EMILY

My friend's heard of him. He says he's very
good.

ABIGAIL

I'm sure he does. But I have a responsibility
in this situation, and I would feel a whole lot
more comfortable with somebody who didn't
just drop in out of the clear blue sky . . .

EMILY

He didn't drop in out of the clear blue sky. He
was recommended by my friend. But even if
we switched lawyers we'd still have to pay him.
But it all comes out of the settlement, so it's
really up to you.

ABIGAIL

No, if you all think he's good . . .

EMILY

I don't know whether he is or not. My friend
thinks he is.

ABIGAIL

All right . . . ! Now Lisa, what is your involve-
ment in all this? What's your angle?

LISA

I just wanted to . . . I was just there.

INT. EMILY'S LIVING ROOM. DAY.

*There are some unpacked boxes stacked in a corner. Monica's stuff
is spread out on the dining room table. Lisa is looking at some of the
photographs. Emily comes out of the kitchen.*

LISA
(*Holding up a photograph*)

Oh my God, is that you?

EMILY

That's me.

LISA

Oh my God. And that's you and Monica,
obviously.

EMILY

Mm hm . . .

LISA
(*Picks up another picture*)

Oh my God, is that her daughter?

EMILY

Mm hm.

LiSA

God . . . So, how old was she when she died?

EMILY

Twelve.

LISA

God. I can't even imagine.

EMILY

Neither could we.

Emily starts packing up some of the photo albums.

LISA

Did you know Monica asked about her, when she was dying?

Pause.

EMILY

No. I didn't.

LISA

Yeah . . . I think she was confused, like she thought I was her daughter for a minute. And

then she was asking me to call her, like to tell
her what happened: You know, like she didn't
remember she was dead?

Emily does not respond.

LISA

But then it got confusing because I said, "Sure,
what's her name?" And she said her name was
Lisa. And I said, "No, that's *my* name." Because
it took me a minute—I didn't realize we had
the same name . . .

Emily does not respond.

LISA

But then when I found out that her daughter
was dead, ever since then I've had this really
strange feeling that in some way, for those last
five minutes, I kind of *was* her daughter. You
know? Like in some weird way this obviously
amazing woman got to be with her daughter
again for a few minutes, right before she died.

EMILY

I see. And is she still inhabiting your body? Or
did she go right back to the spirit world after
it was all over?

LISA

I didn't mean she was literally inhabiting my
body. I don't believe in that stuff at *all* . . .

EMILY

I don't give a fuck *what* you believe in.

LISA

Oh my God! Why are you so mad at me?

EMILY

Because this is not an opera!

LISA
(*Flushing*)

What?

EMILY

I said it's not an opera!

LISA

You think I think this is an *opera?*

EMILY

Yes!

LISA

You think I'm making this into a dramatic situation because I think it's *dramatic?!?*

EMILY

I think you're very young.

LISA

What does that have to do with anything? If anything I think it means I care *more* than someone who's older! Because this kind of thing has never happened to me before!

EMILY

No, it means you care more *easily!* There's a big difference! Except that it's not *you* that it's happening to!

LISA

Yes it is! I know I'm not the one who was run over by a *bus*—!

EMILY

That's right, you weren't. And you're not the one who died of leukemia, and you're not the one who just died in an earthquake in—*Algeria! But you will be.* Do you understand me? *You will be.* And it's not an opera and it's not dramatic—

LISA

I'm well aware of that!

EMILY

And this first-blush phony deepness of yours is worth *nothing.*

LISA

Oh, wow.

EMILY

Do you understand? It's not worth *anything*, because it'll all be troweled over in a month or two. And then when you get older, and you don't have a big reaction every time a *dog* gets run over, *then, then* we'll find out what kind of a person you are! But *this* is *nothing!* I'm sorry, but I didn't start this conversation and I don't play these games.

LISA

I'm not playing *games!*

EMILY

And don't look so outraged! Because I'm not saying anything very outrageous! I'm telling you to knock it off! You have every right to falsify your own life, but you have no right to falsify anyone else's. It's what makes people into *Nazis!* And I'm sorry, but it's a little suspicious that you're making such a fuss about this when you didn't even know her, and you're having troubles with your own mother—

LISA

Oh my *God!*

EMILY

But this is *my* life we're talking about, much more than it is yours! Because it's my *real friend* who got killed, who I'm never going to see again, *really!* Whom I have known since I was nineteen years old myself. OK? And I don't want that sucked into some kind of adolescent self-dramatization!

LISA

I'm not fucking dramatizing anything!

EMILY
(*Not having it*)

OK—

LISA

I was *there*, and you weren't! And if I happen to express myself a little hyperbolically, Emily, that's just the way I talk! I can't help it if my mother is an actress! Why are you being so fucking strident?

EMILY

Strident?

LISA

Yeah.

EMILY

OK. Um, you should leave.

LISA

Why? Because I called you strident?

EMILY

Yeah: Strident? You should leave.

LISA

OK! I will.

EMILY

NOW!

LISA

OK! Let me get my purse!

Lisa grabs her purse and coat. Emily half-walks, half-drives her toward the front door.

LISA

Does this mean we're dropping the whole inquiry?

EMILY

It means you're leaving. I don't know what else it means.

LISA

All I meant by saying you were strident was that you were being emphatic! I obviously misused the word!

EMILY

Look it up when you get home.

LISA

Jesus Christ. You're amazing.

EMILY

Yeah. Uh huh. I'm amazing.

LISA
(*Bursts into tears*)

Why are you *doing* this . . . ?!

EMILY

Lisa, I'm not doing anything! I'm a human being! Monica was a human being! So was her daughter! And so is your mother! We are not supporting characters in the fascinating story of your life!

LISA

I never said or thought you were . . . ! And I really didn't mean to call you strident! I totally misused the word! I wasn't trying to insult you, Emily, I really wasn't! I feel so bad about what happened and I'm trying so hard to do something about it! And I don't understand why if I say something wrong you can't just give me a break! I'm not trying to dramatize anything, Emily. I really know about that trend, and I really don't think I've been doing that . . . !

Emily looks at her for a long moment.

INT. COHEN LIVING ROOM. NIGHT

Lisa, Joan, and Curtis are watching Joan being interviewed on TV. We don't see the screen.

JOAN ON TV (O.C.)

I've been in the theater my whole life and nothing like this has ever happened to me . . .

INTERVIEWER ON TV (O.C.)

Now, any talk of the play becoming a film?

JOAN ON TV (O.C.)

Oh, I'm sure. But I would never get cast in that.
I'm not a movie star.

INTERVIEWER ON TV (O.C.)

But you're a theater star . . .

JOAN ON TV (O.C.)

I don't know about that either . . .

INTERVIEWER ON TV (O.C.)

You are!

JOAN ON TV (O.C.)
(*Charmingly*)

I guess . . . !

JOAN
(*Looking nervously at Lisa*)

Oh God.

Lisa watches the TV, scowling.

INT. COHEN KITCHEN. NIGHT.

Joan is serving Lisa and Curtis dinner.

JOAN

Lisa? Do you think Emily would like to come
see the play? I thought you could both come
and then maybe we could go out afterwards.

LISA

All right. Let me ask her.

JOAN

Dig in everybody . . .

She sits and they start eating.

LISA

I was thinking about spending next year with Dad.

JOAN
(*Shocked*)

Oh?

LISA

Yeah. You're all worried about my grades. They have really good public schools in Santa Monica, and if I officially lived with him, you wouldn't have to worry about my scholarship.

JOAN

Have you talked to him about this?

LISA

We've had some general discussions.

JOAN
(*To Curtis*)

Do you want to go too?

CURTIS

Me?

JOAN

Yeah. Do you want to move to L.A. too?

CURTIS

No.

JOAN

Well, just let me know if you do.

LISA

Why are you being like this?

JOAN

Why am I being like *what*?

LISA

Why are you about to start *crying*?

JOAN

Because it's your *intention* to make me start crying!

LISA

No it's not—

JOAN

You want to move to L.A. Move to L.A.

LISA

But why can't this even be mentioned without you taking it personally? I'm just introducing a possibility!

JOAN

Oh!

Joan upsets everything on the table.

JOAN	LISA
Here's a possibility that you can make your own fucking dinner! Here's a possibility that you can do whatever you want to do, because I don't even care anymore, you heartless little fuckin' bitch!	Jesus Christ! What is *with* you?

LISA

Fine! Keep it up! It really makes me want to stay here!

JOAN

You think *you're* so fucking perfect!?

She breaks another dish and walks out.

LISA

No!

CURTIS

Good one!

LISA

Shut up!

INT. MR. AARON'S APARTMENT. DAY.

Lisa sits on a chair in Mr. Aaron's tiny studio apartment. She takes a sip of coffee.

LISA

Thank you for letting me come over. I don't know who else to talk to.

Mr. Aaron is listening from the sofa, looking very uncomfortable.

MR. AARON

That's all right . . .

LISA

You've always been very sympathetic to my craziness, and I may not show it all the time, but I actually really appreciate it.

MR. AARON

It's no problem, Lisa. What's been going on?

LISA

I just need to talk to somebody who doesn't completely misunderstand who I am. Or not even who I am, but what's going on inside me, or all around me. Sound confused enough? Anyway, for whatever reason, I always felt like we understood each other on some level, even though I'm like a mass of conflicting impulses and you're basically the most grown-up, rational man I know.

MR. AARON

Well . . . I doubt that's actually *true* but thank you . . .

LISA

You seem pretty fuckin' rational to me. Like that seems to be your leading feature. I mean you obviously have a lot of pretty deep feelings . . . So when you're *rational*—just to finish my thought—it's like this really interesting way of governing yourself. And you don't have to get all uncomfortable again: I'm not talking about what you think I'm talking about, because I know that subject is off-limits. I'm talking about your soul, I guess, and how you feel you have to keep it in check all the time by being sensible. Do you know what I'm saying at all?

MR. AARON

Well . . . We all have feelings, Lisa. I happen to believe that who you are comes out of how you deal with those feelings. Somebody makes you mad, you don't just pick up a gun and shoot them . . . Or if you do, that says something about who you are, and how you've been raised . . .

LISA

Well, I don't want to disillusion you, but we happen to be living in a world where that is what people do. More often than not.

MR. AARON

That's not true, Lisa. I think it's very sad that you see it that way. There's seven billion people alive in the world and you think they don't all want to kill someone once in a while? But they don't. Most of them. Or they see some person . . . (*Pause*) I think most people do try to be civilized by some standard. Even if it's a standard you and I might not agree with . . .

LISA

No, I get it. That's actually the most hopeful thing anybody's said to me for a long time. I don't know why I take such a dire view of things, I really don't.

She removes her jacket. She's wearing a small clingy T-shirt.

LISA

Just a little hot . . . A little *warm* . . . Is this all right?

MR. AARON

Sure.

LISA

Do you allow smoking in your apartment?

MR. AARON

You can smoke.

She gets up, gets her cigarettes out of her purse, and lights one. He brings her an ashtray. They meet at the sofa and sit. Silence.

LISA

I like your apartment.

MR. AARON

Thank you . . . It's actually a sublet . . .

She blows some smoke out and waves it away.

LISA

Sorry.

MR. AARON

That's all right.

Silence.

LISA

This is terrible.

MR. AARON

What is? What's terrible?

LISA

I just like you so much . . . (*Stubs out her cigarette*) Sorry. What a moron.

MR. AARON

(*Taking her hand*)

Hey. Lisa. I'm your friend. And that's not gonna change. That's not gonna change.

LISA

Thanks. Thank you.

She kisses his hand a couple of times.

MR. AARON

Lisa . . .

LISA

Please just let me for a second. I like you *so much.* I like you so, so much.

She settles her head onto his shoulder, holding his hand. They sit like that for a long moment, and then she turns her head gently so she is looking right at him. Another long pause.

LISA

What's it like in Indiana?

MR. AARON

It's OK.

They kiss. It gradually intensifies. Mr. Aaron pulls back.

MR. AARON

OK, look . . .

LISA

Please don't stop me yet . . .

They kiss some more. She puts her hands on him. He stops resisting.

INT. MR. AARON'S APARTMENT. LATER.

They are at his front door. She is in her coat. He is burning with guilt and shame.

LISA

All I can say is I better get a pretty fuckin' good grade in geometry this year. (*Pause*) Lighten up! I'm kidding.

MR. AARON

Sorry. I really didn't expect anything like this to happen. I'm really not sure how to react.

Lisa is stung.

LISA

Don't worry. I'm not gonna tell anybody. If that's what you're worried about. I totally initiated the whole thing. Anyway, it's just sex. You're acting like a little kid. I'll see you in school.

She opens the door and walks out. He is very flummoxed.

MR. AARON
(*To himself*)

You're a fuckin' idiot.

He locks the door.

KIRSTEN V.O.

I think that teenagers should definitely rule
the world . . .

Kirsten's voice takes us into—

INT. HISTORY CLASS. DAY.

*"SHOULD TEENAGERS RULE THE WORLD? YES/NO?" is writ-
ten in big letters on the BLACKBOARD.*

KIRSTEN

. . . because teenagers aren't corrupted by
adult life yet, and they're idealists, and they
care. And I know a lot of people feel that teenagers are really naive, which they are, many of
them. But they still haven't had a chance to
get burned out by the disappointments and
the harsh realities of learning how to play the
game. So yes, I would vote yes.

KLEIN

All right: Lisa?

Lisa starts to speak—

MOMENTS LATER—Lisa and Angie are arguing fervidly.

ANGIE

—and I'm not even going to comment on the
fact that you just compared a 19-year-old Pal-
estinian to a member of the Hitler Youth—

ANGIE

—which I personally find so
offensive I don't even know
where to start—Oh, it's not
because they've been oc-
cupied and humiliated and
bombed out of their homes
for the last
fifty years?

LEWIS

Come on, guys . . . Raise
your hands!

KLEIN

One at a time!

LISA

That's right. Because they
both like to kill Jews.

KLEIN

Hey! Hey! Lisa! Hey!

LISA

Yes! That's partly why they
like it! It's not like killing
civilians is their last resort!
It's their first resort because
it's easy and they *like* it!

ANGIE

Oh they *like* it? They're just bad people and they *like* it?

LISA

Yes! There *are* bad people in the world! I think they *liked*
blowing up the World Trade Center! They kill their own
sisters when they get *raped!* It's called *barbarism!*

MONICA

Who kills their own sisters?

LIONEL

You guys are not the only
ones in this class!

LISA

It's practically all people *do*
is kill each other! If they
didn't like it they wouldn't
do it! Period!

LEWIS

Lisa!

ANGIE

You're not even Jewish, Lisa!

LISA

I'm fuckin' half-Jewish, and who cares what I am? I'm anti-murder, not pro-Israel.

KLEIN

The next Goddamn person who opens their mouth without raising their hand is outta this class!

LEWIS

Lisa? Lisa! You can leave!

LISA

Fine. Thank you.

Lisa grabs her bag and gets up to leave.

INT. THEATER LOBBY. NIGHT.

Ramon applauds as Joan comes into the lobby where he, Lisa, and Emily are waiting for her after the play.

INT. RESTAURANT. NIGHT.

Joan, Lisa, Emily, and Ramon are at a table, having drinks.

LISA

—and I guess I lost my cool a little . . .

JOAN

But who is running these discussions . . . ?

LISA	RAMON
. . . but there is such a thing as—	But Lisa, you have to remember, it's always easy for the dominant side to be content with the status quo.

Pause.

JOAN

Mmm.

EMILY

How do you mean, Ramon?

RAMON

I mean the oppressor is always in favor of law and order because it's his law and his order. He uses violence to maintain his position and calls it the rule of law. But when the person underfoot uses violence to change his status, he's called a criminal and a terrorist, and the violence of the State is called upon to put him down, and once again it's called the rule of law. In Colombia—

EMILY

I see. And what would you like them to do?

Pause.

RAMON

"They" meaning—

EMILY

The Jew oppressors. What would you like them
to do?

Pause.

RAMON   EMILY

I didn't use that expression.   No, you didn't.
But since you ask—

LISA

Um, I just spent the whole day arguing about
this: I didn't really mean to bring it up again.

EMILY
(*Turns on her*)

Don't *handle* me.

LISA

I'm not handling you.

JOAN
(*Generally*)

What did you think of the play?

RAMON   LISA

And I think it's ironic in the   Don't bother, Mom.
extreme that the victims of
Nazis find it essential to use   EMILY
the Nazi tactics to sustain
their occupation.   If the Israelis were like Nazis
                                   there wouldn't be any Arabs
                                   left. And I'm leaving.

LISA
(*Agreeing with Emily*)

That's what *I* think!

Emily tries to unhook her purse from the back of her chair.

JOAN

That seems excessive, Emily, come on—

RAMON

That's the response. That's the Jewish response.

EMILY

It's the what?

RAMON

It's the Jewish response. You don't like what I
am saying or what I do, so you—

Emily throws her drink in his face.

EMILY

That's *my* Jewish response.

Emily walks out.

JOAN

Oh my God . . . !

RAMON

It's all right . . . (*Wiping off his face*) That's
all right . . . It's a perfect little . . . encap-
sule . . . It's the Jewish response.

There is a horrible silence as Joan and Lisa watch Ramon clean his shirt.

INT. JOAN'S ROOM. NIGHT.

Joan is getting ready for bed. Lisa appears in the doorway.

> LISA
>
> Sorry about all that tonight.

> JOAN
>
> Yeah. Your friend is a delight.

> LISA
>
> Emily's a really passionate person. She really cares about things.

> JOAN
>
> She's *rude*, Lisa. Ramon was my guest, not hers. And so was she, as a matter of fact—

> LISA
>
> So what? Why is it so important that people be *polite* all the time? Why is *that* the big priority?

> JOAN
>
> No—I'm not ar—I'm not arguing about this with you! I'm not interested in an exchange of ideas. As it happens Ramon said a few thingshappens Ramon said a few things I wasn't too crazy about either, so I guess that's the end of that . . .

LISA

Oh is that supposed to be Emily's fault too?

JOAN

I don't want to talk to you right now. Please go away.

INT. RAMON'S APARTMENT. NIGHT.

Ramon is on the phone, pacing slowly back and forth.

RAMON
(*On the phone*)

Joan, I won't defend myself. All that I meant was, that was the typical response you will get from someone who will take that position that that woman was taking. But if you like to break up with me because I used the wrong adjective, what I'm going to do? I'm not going to beg you.

INT. COHEN KITCHEN/KARL'S HOUSE. DAY.

Lisa is eating a snack and looks up as Joan enters slowly and checks the water on the stove without speaking.

The PHONE RINGS. Lisa picks up.

LISA

Hello?

KARL
(*On phone*)

Yeah. It's Dad.

INT. KARL'S HOUSE. DAY.

WE CUT BETWEEN THEM.

> LISA
>
> Hi, Dad, how are you? I'm really looking forward to our horseback riding trip . . .

> KARL
>
> Yeah. That's why I'm calling. I don't think it's going to happen.

> LISA
>
> Really? What's the matter?

> KARL
>
> Nothing's the matter. Nobody seems to really want to go, and I don't really feel like spending three thousand bucks on something nobody has the slightest interest in. So I think it's obviously better for everyone if we just cancel.

> LISA
>
> I never said I didn't want to go.

> KARL
>
> Well, I can't seem to get a straight answer about what anybody wants to eat. Um, Annette is giving me a hard time about her schedule, I talk to Curtis and all I get are monosyllables, so—

> LISA
>
> I think he's really looking forward to it—

KARL

I don't think *anybody's* looking forward to it . . . !

Lisa does not respond.

KARL

OK? (*Pause*) *I* don't want to go. Also . . . I, uh, I also think it would be good to shelve the idea of your coming out here next year. It looks like things are gonna start picking up for me in the fall, which means I'm probably not gonna be around the house all that much, and since you and Annette detest each other, I don't, uh, I don't think that's what I want to come home to after a fourteen hour day.

LISA

We don't detest each other—

KARL

OK, well, it doesn't really strike me as something you're that serious about anyway, so what do you say we just table it for the time being?

LISA

OK.

KARL

OK. So tell Curtis, uh, that New Mexico's off . . . Ummm, and I will talk to you, ummm, whenever.

LISA

OK.

KARL

Yeah.

He hangs up. Lisa hangs up too.

JOAN

What's wrong?

LISA

Dad's cancelling the trip.

JOAN

What? Why?

LISA

He's says nobody wants to go and he doesn't want to spend the money.

JOAN

Did you say you didn't want to go?

LISA

No, I know there was some problem with Annette about arranging for food because I don't eat dead animals, but I didn't think it was going to wreck the whole trip.

JOAN

Oh boy.

LISA

I thought you said it sounded like it was going to be a disaster. Personally I'm relieved. I'm not moving out there, either, by the way, obviously. Which is fine too.

She miserably resumes eating. Joan looks on.

INT. KARL'S HOUSE. DAY.

Karl sits holding the phone in a savage depression.

INT. DEUTSCH OFFICE. DAY.

INSERT: A NEW YORK TIMES *METRO SECTION ARTICLE, lying on Deutsch's DESK:*

> "DRIVER IN BUS CRASH HAD RECORD OF PREVIOUS ACCIDENTS. *The driver of a city bus which killed an Upper West Side woman last month had two previous driving violations on his record, according to . . .*"

Over this we HEAR Deutsch on the telephone.

DEUTSCH (O.C.)

Dr. Berger . . . The man is not experiencing discomfort, he's in *pain* . . . Well, I use the *real* word . . . Uh huh? His other knee is eighty-seven years old too, OK? So I'm not all that impressed with your diagnosis. OK? . . . OK: I'm gonna have to call you back.

Deutsch hangs up, goes to the door and opens it.

DEUTSCH

Ladies? Come on in. I'm sorry.

Emily and Lisa come in. He shuts the door.

EMILY

Russell.

DEUTSCH

Hey Lisa.

LISA

Hi.

DEUTSCH

Well, they want to settle.

LISA

They do?

EMILY

They do?

INT. DEUTSCH'S OFFICE/INT. ABIGAIL'S HOUSE. LATER.

*Lisa, Emily, and Deutsch sit around the SPEAKER PHONE, talking
to Abigail and her husband, ROB BERWITZ. We don't see the Berwitzes,
we just hear their voices.*

ABIGAIL
(*On the speaker phone*)

Mr. Deutsch? Mr. Deutsch—

DEUTSCH

I'm right here.

ABIGAIL

Mr. Deutsch—I'm just gonna give my husband the floor—

ROB
(*On the speaker phone*)

I just had the thought—

ROB

Mr. Deutsch, I had the give thought, if they're willing to settle so quickly, maybe we're better off waiting a little bit, maybe rattling the sabre a little bit more . . .

ABIGAIL

Yes, if they're so quick to agree to a settlement on this basis—

DEUTSCH
(*On "settlement"*)

What you gotta realize—What you gotta really—

EMILY

Abigail, Russel doesn't think—Sorry, go ahead.

DEUTSCH

No, no . . .

ABIGAIL

But if they responded so strongly based on *one story* . . .

ROB

Maybe we're cuttin' our own throats here.

DEUTSCH

They *are* responding to the story in the paper . . .

ABIGAIL

. . . That's just common sense.

DEUTSCH

But what you gotta understand is they're offering to settle now because they want to get the story *out* of the paper.

EMILY

That's why Russell thinks—

ABIGAIL

I'm sorry—

LISA

Besides, the main point is not to jack up the *price.*

ROB

We didn't hear that last.

DEUTSCH
(*To Emily and Lisa*)

Ladies, let me just—Abigail. Rob. If I could finish my thought: They're jumping at the bait right now, but if another six months goes by, we run a serious risk of losing our momentum. You see what I mean? Now, I'm gonna hit them very, very hard, I guarantee you. That's why I wanted all of us together on the phone, so we could talk about your other terms, besides the damages. I promise you, I'm gonna be very, very aggressive—

ABIGAIL

What other terms would there be?

ROB

What do you mean, like some kind of a fund?

DEUTSCH

A what?

ROB

Some kind of fund? For the kids?

DEUTSCH

I don't understand what you mean by a fund . . .

ROB
(*To Abigail*)

What does he mean, "besides the damages"?

EMILY

What fuckin' fund?

ABIGAIL

Mr. Deutsch? Do you mean some kind of trust fund, a fund that would be set up by the bus company for our kids? For tax purposes?

LISA

I have no idea.

ABIGAIL

Because I have to tell you we have just lived through that nightmare with Monica and our children, and it was not a pleasant experience.

We just want a clean, straight—damages is fine. We'll pay the taxes on it. At least we'll have something in our hand . . .

DEUSTCH	LISA
I don't really know what kind of fund you're talking about . . .	We're not talking about— Hello? We're talking about—Hello?

Pause.

ABIGAIL

We're still here.

LISA

We're talking about the *driver*. Getting the driver fired—

ABIGAIL	LISA
Oh, yes—	—as part of the conditions.

ABIGAIL

Oh yes. Absolutely. If you think he's at fault—

ROB

Just as long as they don't think they can buy us off just by gettin' rid of this guy. You see what I mean?

DEUTSCH

Absolutely.

ABIGAIL	ROB
Absolutely. If they're so quick to agree—	But you see what I mean? What we're most concerned about here is the amount.

EMILY

Yes, we're getting that, Rob.

INT. COHEN APARTMENT—LIVING ROOM. DAY.

Lisa is still in her coat; she has just told Joan the news. Joan is holding some newspapers.

JOAN

Lisa, I'm really proud of you.

LISA

Thank you.

JOAN

Really, really proud . . . !

LISA

Thank you.

Pause. Joan resumes tidying up the living room.

JOAN

So what happens now?

LISA

They have to figure out the terms.

JOAN

Uh huh?

The PHONE RINGS. Joan picks it up.

JOAN
(*Into phone*)

Hello? . . . Yes . . . *What do you mean?*

LISA

What's the matter?

JOAN
(*Listening*)

Yes? . . . Yes? (*To Lisa*) Ramon had a heart
attack.

LISA

What? Is he gonna be—

JOAN

Quiet!

*Lisa takes a step back. Curtis appears. They both watch Joan on the
phone. Joan listens, straightens up, and calms herself while the person
on the phone talks.*

JOAN

OK . . . OK . . . Let me write that down.

EXT. RIVERSIDE CHAPEL. DAY.

*Well-dressed mourners are going inside the Upper West Side funeral
parlor.*

INT. FUNERAL PARLOR. DAY.

It is very full of people. A variety of languages are being spoken—mostly English, but lots of Spanish, some French, and one or two others. Joan and Lisa look around the room. They speak in low, hushed tones.

LISA

Do you know any of these people?

JOAN

No . . . He never introduced me to any of his friends . . .

LISA

OK, I'm really not trying to be funny, but isn't this a Jewish funeral home?

JOAN

I guess they do both.

They notice several good-looking women scattered around the room, several of them on their own, crying a little too hard. Lisa and Joan look at each other.

RODRIGO, a handsome, slender kid of 20, comes up to Joan. His accent is British, with a slight Colombian cadence.

RODRIGO

Excuse me. Joan?

JOAN

Yes. Oh you must be Rodrigo. Oh my God, oh I'm so sorry.

She impulsively embraces him.

JOAN

Rodrigo, this is my—

RODRIGO

I want to tell you, Joan, my dad talked about you all the time.

JOAN

He did?

RODRIGO

Yes. The night he met you, he called me in England and woke me to tell me about it, he was so excited. I never heard him talk about anyone like that since my mother died.

JOAN

Really.

RODRIGO

I don't know if this is appropriate, but . . .

JOAN

No, it's OK . . . !

RODRIGO

. . . he went out a lot . . . (*Pause*) But, the last time I spoke to him, he told me from the moment he met you, he knew he wanted to marry you. Because for the first time since he lost my mother, he finally met a woman he could really connect with.

JOAN
(*At a total loss*)

Well—Well—Well, he was a very sweet man. And I know he loved you and your brother very much.

RODRIGO
(*Getting tearful*)

Yeah, I know he did. Thank you. Excuse me.

Rodrigo goes to greet some relatives who are arriving.

INT. LISA'S ROOM. DAY.

Lisa is at her computer. Joan is by the doorway.

JOAN

Thanks for coming with me today. I really appreciate it.

LISA

Oh, you're welcome.

JOAN

I don't want to be macabre, but Ramon and I were supposed to go to hear *The Tales of Hoffman* the week after next and I still have the tickets. Would you be interested in going? Or should I give them away?

LISA

Um, I'll go.

JOAN

OK. It's Monday night. We can dress up.

LISA

OK.

Pause.

JOAN

What did you *make* of that?

LISA

People don't relate to each other, Mom. They're totally disconnected. That's what I make of it.

JOAN

Well . . . I think it's pretty unfortunate that you think that. Because I feel like you and I used to relate to each other really well.

LISA

I'm not trying to hurt your feelings. It's just a general observation.

JOAN

OK . . . Hey, could I get a hug?

LISA

Sure.

Lisa rises and hugs Joan. It's not a good hug. They break apart.

INT. LISA'S BATHROOM. NIGHT.

Lisa looks at a pregnancy test stick. Both lines are red.

LATER—Joan is looking at the same little stick, while Lisa waits.

JOAN

OK. What do you want to do?

LISA

What do you mean? Aren't
you going to *tell* me what to
do? (*Half-laughing*) Baby . . . ?

JOAN

It's your body. It's your baby.
What do you want to do?

JOAN

Yes! Now who is the father?

LISA

It could be a lot of people.

Joan looks at her. Lisa haltingly holds her ground. Joan takes a sympathetic step toward her. Lisa shrinks back. Joan stops. Her expression hardens.

JOAN

Who.

LISA

I'm never gonna tell you, Mom! It's against my
principles! Such as they are.

> JOAN
> (*On "such"*)

No, but you want to send that bus driver to jail
for running a red light! And you won't tell me
about these boys?

INT. GYNECOLOGISTS' OFFICES/WAITING ROOM. NIGHT.

*Joan waits. She looks around the small room. There are two couples
and a lone woman around Joan's age, all waiting. The receptionists
chat and answer the phones. A doctor passes by. A NURSE appears.*

> NURSE

Mrs. Cohen?

*TRACKING JOAN as she gets up and follows the Nurse down a
hall . . .*

> NURSE

. . . she's still a little woozy from the anaes-
thetic . . .

*Joan goes into the recovery room. Lisa is on the table in a crumpled
paper robe, looking like a crumpled piece of paper herself. Joan sits
down.*

> LISA

Hi.

> JOAN

Hi, honey.

LISA

I'm sorry, Mom.

JOAN

Let's talk about it later.

Silence.

EXT. STREET. DOWNTOWN. DAY

Lisa walks down the street with determination. She stops short at a red light and has to wait while the traffic goes by.

INT. DEUTSCH'S OFFICE. DAY.

Deutsch sits with Emily and Lisa. The Berwitzes are on the SPEAKER PHONE.

DEUTSCH

I'm very pleased to be able to inform you all that I had a long meeting with the lawyer for the bus company, and they've agreed to settle out of court for three hundred and fifty thousand dollars.

ABIGAIL & ROB

What! Fantastic! That's wonderful!

DEUTSCH

I'm assuming this is agreeable to everybody—

ABIGAIL

Yes, fantastic.

ROB

That is fantastic!

DEUTSCH

But I gotta—obviously I gotta bring the offer to you, get your approval—

ROB

Mr. Deutsch . . . ?

DEUTSCH

Now, I know there was a concern after our last call that we were jumping the gun a little bit—

ROB

That's OK—

ABIGAIL

We're only—

EMILY

Abigail? Rob? If we could just listen to what Russell has to say, and then talk about it once he's told us the whole story and given us his recommendation . . .

ROB

Yes. Sorry. Fire away.

DEUTSCH

I was gonna say: I know there was a concern after our last call that we were jumping the gun a little bit—

ROB

That's OK—

ABIGAIL

We were just—

EMILY

Would you let him talk please?!

DEUTSCH

It's OK.

ABIGAIL

We're sorry.

DEUTSCH

I want to tell you I think it's a very good offer.
I think they're very anxious to settle, but I also
do think that at this moment they're under the
maximum amount of pressure we can really
bring to bear, and I don't believe they're gonna
come up any higher—

ABIGAIL

Hey. Three hundred and fifty thousand dollars . . .

ROB

OK, now let me just—

ABIGAIL

. . . that's nothin' to sneeze at.

ROB	ABIGAIL
I just want to introduce the thought—	Now, *I* think—Can you all hear me?

DEUTSCH, EMILY, LISA

Yes!

ABIGAIL

Yeow! Was that everybody? OK:

LISA

What about—

ABIGAIL

—Emily? What do you think?

EMILY

I think it sounds like we should do it . . .

EMILY

But I'd like to discuss—

ABIGAIL

Hey, if that's the vote . . .

ROB

Unless you think there's something to be gained from holding out for more.

DEUTSCH

I think it would be a big mistake.

ABIGAIL

Robbie, what do you think?

ROB

Sold!

ABIGAIL

Sold!

DEUTSCH

OK. Now the only down side to this as it stands—and the reason I asked Emily and Lisa to be here is because I know this may be a serious wrinkle for you all—is that the bus company will absolutely not discuss the removal of the driver.

LISA

What? What do you *mean?*

EMILY

What?

ROB

The driver?

LISA

Then *forget* it. Tell them to *forget* it.

EMILY

What do you mean they won't discuss the removal of the driver?

DEUTSCH

Please. Ladies. Let me finish what I'm saying.

ROB

Whoa—hello!

ABIGAIL

It's just a blast in our *ears.*

EMILY
(*To Lisa*)

Let him finish.

LISA

Finish what? *Forget* it!

DEUTSCH
(To Emily)

Thank you. I want you to understand, Lisa, I pressed them very, very hard on this, but they will not discuss disciplining a company employee as part of the settlement because it could be seen as an admission of guilt on the part of the MTA—

LISA

What does giving us three hundred thousand dollars mean?

DEUTSCH

Settling out of court does not imply an admission of guilt. It simply does not carry the same stigma. On top of that, you may not know, Lisa, they're involved in a very tricky labor dispute at the MTA right now:

LISA

Yeah, we know all about that! Just tell them to forget it.

DEUTSCH

I know that's *your* reaction . . .

LISA

It's the only reason we're *here*.

ROB

Can I jump in here? Russell?

DEUTSCH

. . . but it's really not your decision.

ROB   ABIGAIL

Hello? Are you still   Please!
with us?

LISA

It's Emily's decision.

EMILY

No.

DEUTSCH

No.

ROB   LISA

Hello?   It's not?

ABIGAIL   DEUTSCH

They're not listening,   It's Abigail's decision.
Robbie.   Because she's the next of
                                                         kin.

LISA

But she didn't even *know* about it!

EMILY

That doesn't matter.

ABIGAIL

Could we get back in this conversation please?

DEUTSCH

Yes. I'm sorry. Obviously there's some very strong emotions going either way on this—

ABIGAIL

Listen, Emily? I don't know what you're think-ing, but Rob and I are thinking we should take Russell's recommendation while we can. Be-cause if they won't fire the guy, they're not gonna fire him. And six months or a year from now, we're gonna—

ROB

Exactly.

ABIGAIL

—we're gonna be in a situation where we're beggin' them for half this much—

LISA

The entire point of the lawsuit was to get the guy fired so he doesn't kill somebody *else*—!

DEUTSCH

Lemme just clarify—

LISA

—it was *not* to get you three hundred and fifty thousand dollars you didn't know you were en-titled to, for somebody you didn't even *like* . . . !

ABIGAIL

This is a distortion—

LISA

And the only reason you're getting the money at all is because *I* started this whole fucking thing in motion! I'm sorry for swearing, but you should be willing to trade in *all* the money for getting this guy off the *street*—!

EMILY

For *getting* him, Abigail!

ABIGAIL

Well I'm sorry, but I have a responsibility to Monica, and I take that responsibility very seriously. And rather than being abused over the telephone and cursed at for having the courtesy to involve you in these discussions, Lisa, I would hope you would be guided by our judgement. Unless I'm wrong about that.

LISA

None of that matters—

ABIGAIL

Unless I'm *wrong* about that! Just what is your *interest* in this?

LISA

Because *I'm* the one who killed her! *I'm* the one who killed her! But at least I know I did it, and that guy has no idea! And he's wandering around blaming everybody else and all I want is for somebody to let him know that what he did was wrong! And if they don't fire him and all you want is the money and the police won't do anything, how is he gonna know he's wrong? You can't take the deal, Abigail! It wasn't so you could get any money, it was because we wanted to get him fired!

ABIGAIL

Well it may not matter to *you*, but where I come from, three hundred and fifty thousand dollars is an awful lot of money, and to my mind is a positive result of all this tragedy and not just negative. Not just getting someone fired for one mistake, no matter how bad it was—

LISA

Oh SHOVE IT UP YOUR ASS!

She knocks the speaker phone off the desk and runs to the door in floods of tears.

DEUTSCH & EMILY

Lisa!

LISA

You sleazy fucking lawyer! And you're a moralistic cunt!

She runs out.

EXT. CITY HALL PARK. DAY.

Looking down from the 30th floor we see Lisa running across the street toward the subway station.

EXT. UPPER WEST SIDE—BROADWAY. DAY.

Lisa comes up out of the 86th Street subway station into the afternoon crowd and runs to the curb. She stops for the light. A city bus appears down the street and passes by. She cranes her neck to see the drivers face. It's not Maretti. Lisa runs across the street.

EXT. SCHOOL. DAY.

Lisa stands against a car, smoking. The kids flow out of the building. Mr. Aaron comes out, talking with Bonnie, the gymnastics teacher. They walk away from the school together. Lisa catches up with them.

> BONNIE

Hey, Lisa. What's up?

> LISA

Hey, did you guys know I had an abortion last week?

Pause.

> MR. AARON

No. I didn't know that.

> LISA

Yeah, it cost four hundred dollars.

Pause.

> BONNIE

Um, should I . . .

MR. AARON

No, no, don't go anywhere.

LISA

Yeah, don't go anywhere.

Bonnie doesn't know what to make of this. Mr. Aaron looks steadily at Lisa.

MR. AARON

Do you want to tell us about it?

LISA

Yeah. I do.

MR. AARON

OK. Go ahead.

LISA

Well . . .

She doesn't speak. Pause.

MR. AARON

It's OK. Go ahead.

She still can't speak.

MR. AARON

Go ahead.

Pause.

BONNIE

Do your parents know about this, Lisa?

LISA

Yes.

BONNIE

Have you told the father, honey?

LISA

No . . . There's a couple of people it could be.

MR. AARON

Well, I think you better tell them. Whoever they are.

LISA

No . . . No . . . Never mind . . . I'm sure he's sorry anyway, whichever one he is.

MR. AARON

I don't see how that makes any difference—if he's sorry. That doesn't matter.

Pause.

LISA

I'm sorry. I—This is really embarassing—I shouldn't have brought this up. Please don't tell anyone.

BONNIE

We're not gonna tell anyone—

BONNIE	LISA
—but you're gonna have to tell whoever it could be—	That's OK. I gotta go. Thanks for listening. It's—It doesn't matter about the father, because the whole thing was my fault.

She shakes her head, turns, and hurries away.

BONNIE

What was *that . . . ?*

Mr. Aaron does not respond. He watches Lisa walk away.

INT. COHEN APARTMENT. DAY.

Lisa comes in. Curtis is practicing the piano.

CURTIS

Mom's looking for you.

LISA

What for?

CURTIS

She thinks you're going out with her tonight.

LISA

Where are we going?

CURTIS

I don't know.

EXT. BROADWAY. NIGHT.

Lisa and Joan are nicely dressed up for the opera. They are looking for a taxi. Lisa steps off the curb. Joan catches her sleeve.

> JOAN

Don't get run over!

A CAB SPEEDS BY. They step back. Lisa looks up the street. A CITY BUS is approaching.

> LISA

Wait. I want to see if that's him.

> JOAN

What.

They wait. The bus comes closer, heading straight toward them. Lisa grabs her mother's arm.

> LISA

It is him. Mom, that's the one . . .

Maretti is driving the bus. Joan and Lisa look at him as he approaches. He's staring out ahead, then he sees Lisa and Joan. He can't see their faces and doesn't recognize Lisa: He just sees two dolled-up women under the street light. He smiles at them as he drives by.

Joan looks at Lisa. Lisa looks like she's about to throw up.

> JOAN

Come on, sweetheart . . .

Lisa does not respond. Joan hails a taxi.

EXT. METROPOLITAN OPERA—MEZZANINE TERRACE. NIGHT.

Lisa is out on the terrace, smoking a cigarette and looking out over Lincoln Center. Joan comes out and stands next to her, but Lisa won't look at her or interact.

> JOAN
>
> Well, so far it's not the greatest opera I ever heard.

> LISA
>
> What do you mean? It's OK.

Pause. Joan turns and goes back inside.

The end-of-intermission chimes sound. People start going in. Lisa keeps smoking. At the last minute, she throws her cigarette away and hurries inside.

INT. METROPOLITAN OPERA—GRAND STAIRCASE. NIGHT

Lisa comes down the curving staircase and goes into—

INT. METROPOLITAN OPERA, AUDITORIUM—ORCHESTRA. NIGHT.

Lisa hurries down the long aisle. The LIGHTS DIM. The audience applauds the entering conductor. She picks her way past the other patrons in the row and takes her seat just as the MUSIC STARTS. Joan looks at her. Lisa stares straight ahead.

The curtain rises. On the stage, the mezzo-soprano and the soprano start to sing the Barcarolle. It's very beautiful.

Joan looks next to her at Lisa. Lisa is trying not to cry, but tears are dripping slowly down her face. She sniffs and wipes them away, but they keep coming. Joan looks at her again, but Lisa still won't look at her. Joan looks straight forward again.

Suddenly Lisa takes Joan's hand. Joan turns, startled. Lisa breaks down completely. Joan squeezes Lisa's hand. Lisa squeezes back and Joan starts crying too.

As the duet goes on, Joan and Lisa sit side by side, holding hands, Lisa crying and holding on tight, wiping her eyes with her free hand; Joan crying too, but not as hard, grateful finally that the spell has been broken.

The duet ends. CUT TO BLACK.

THE END

Acknowledgments

A screenplay is so closely linked to the film it eventually becomes that it is sometimes difficult to separate the people who helped you with the script from those who helped you make the movie. For the film itself, the production credits cover everyone to whom I am most indebted: the cast, designers, editors, and crew. All the people, in short, who actually turned the screenplay into a movie. But there are a few other people I need to mention. Naturally, there is some overlap.

Patsy Broderick, Matthew Broderick, J. Smith-Cameron, Elaine May, Stanley Donen, Mark Ruffalo, Josh Hamilton, Alexis Neumann, Ann Roth, Lily Thorne, Pippin Parker, Kim Parker, Tiffany Parker, Andy Yerkes, and many other friends and colleagues gave me help and insight into the construction of the story at various stages in its development, all of which were crucial to my understanding what I was trying to write, film, and edit.

Tiffany Parker was my assistant throughout the preproduction and production process. Her genius for organization and for getting things done quickly and efficiently, her gentle and sensitive nature, and her perfect tact gave me a support without which I simply could not have managed. Kim Parker brought her equally remarkable talents and temperament to guiding and organizing the editing process when it became more complex and daunting than anyone could have possibly foreseen. I'm eternally beholden to both of them.

I cannot really express how grateful I am to Renée Fleming, Susan Graham, and Christine Goerke for appearing in the opera sequences of the movie. Of course no screenplay can begin to convey in any sense the contribution they made to the film. And I can honestly say that the days they worked for us and sang for us were easily among the happiest, most bedazzled days of my life. To watch the entire film crew melt into the sheer shock of beauty that radiated from their voices and flowed over everybody and everything, all the lights, cables, equipment, and general detritus of a movie set, take after take, was like watching the grueling, silly difficulties of filmmaking dissolve into a stream of music and light. I still can't believe they were in the movie at all.

Marty Scorsese gave me his support, his time, his help, his eye, his ear, his voice, and the benefit of his genius with a generosity of spirit and action that I can never sufficiently repay or thank him for enough, though I have tried. I owe the same oversized debt, in short order, to Thelma Schoonmaker, Emma Tillinger Koskoff, Matt Damon, Matthew Rosengart, Scott Brock, Matthew Broderick—again—and my uncredited but irreplaceable third editor, Anthony Ripoli.

Finally, I don't believe I would still be on my feet without J. and without my parents. And of course without Nelly, there would be hardly any point to anything. Darling of all darlings, I probably owe you most of all. But to you I can hopefully give something back in the years to come.